BE MORE HUMAN

-By Akshat Tiwari

BlueRose ONE.com
Stories Matter
NewDelhi • London

BLUEROSE PUBLISHERS
India | U.K.

For permissions requests or inquiries regarding this publication, please contact:

BLUEROSE PUBLISHERS
www.BlueRoseONE.com
info@bluerosepublishers.com
+91 8882 898 898
+4407342408967

ISBN: 978-93-7542-956-2

First Edition: March 2026

Hey! I am Akshat a computer science engineer on paper.

An entrepreneur in practice. But if I'm being honest, I'm mostly just someone who can't stop noticing things.

Like the way people say they want one thing but choose another. The way attention gets pulled so easily.
The way life quietly nudges us and we call it "my decision."

I build ventures. I love building. The chaos, the late nights, the figuring-it-out energy. But somewhere between code and conversations, I started paying attention to something else the invisible structure underneath it all.

Incentives | Ego | Fear | Validation | Control.

Have you ever caught yourself reacting to something and thought, "Wait… why did I do that?" That question stays with me. Over time, you start seeing the same patterns everywhere. In relationships. In ambition. Even in your own thoughts. And it's not dramatic. It's subtle. Almost quiet. That's what makes it powerful.

I'm not here to act like I've figured life out. I really haven't. I'm still confused half the time. Still learning. Still unlearning. But I've spent enough time observing to know that most of us feel the same things we just don't always say them out loud.

So, this book? It's not a lecture. It's not a masterplan. It's more like me texting you when something clicks. Or sitting across from you and saying, "Okay, listen… I've been thinking about something."

No pressure. No superiority. Just honesty.

Think of it as two people trying to understand the same strange world and being real about it.

BEFORE WE BEGIN

You don’t need to rush through this book.
You don’t need to read it in any particular way.

Some parts may feel familiar.
Some may take time to settle.

That’s part of reading, not something to correct.
This book isn’t here to convince you of anything.

It isn’t asking you to change or adopt a system.
It’s simply a place to pause and notice.

Read at your own pace.
Stop when something stays with you.

Move on when it doesn’t.
If a thought feels obvious, sit with it a little longer.

Familiar things often carry more than they first appear to.

Take what feels true to you.
Leave the rest without effort.

Our way to

BE MORE HUMAN

starts with

Breathe.

Why This?

This book exists because life keeps moving, and something in you hasn't caught up. You do what needs to be done.

You handle things. You make decisions. Nothing is falling apart.

From the outside, everything looks manageable.
That's why it's hard to explain what feels off.

So, you don't explain it.
You keep going.

But effort costs more than it used to. Rest doesn't reset you the same way. Days move efficiently, but not deeply. There's no clear reason for it, and that's what makes it difficult.

If something were obviously wrong, you could fix it. Instead, you adjust yourself.

You become more controlled. More careful. You learn what works and repeat it. Life starts functioning smoothly on the surface. And slowly, almost without noticing, you begin living slightly outside yourself.

You don't fall apart.
You thin out.

You notice it when progress doesn't register. When conversations end and nothing stays with you. When staying busy feels safer than slowing down.

You assume this is maturity.
You assume everyone else is managing better.
So, you keep going. This book isn't here because something is broken.
It's here because a lot of people are carrying lives that work, but don't quite fit.

They're meeting expectations without knowing when those expectations became theirs.
This book doesn't explain that.
It doesn't name it.
It just notices it.
If something here feels familiar, that's enough.
That's why this exists.

ACT I
(Clear Vision)

The Foundation Most People Skip

Most people try to fix their thinking before they understand what their thinking is supposed to serve.

They work on clarity. They practice mindfulness. They journal, meditate, analyse, strategize. They consume content about mental discipline, emotional regulation, cognitive restructuring. They are deeply invested in improving how they think.

But they never stop to ask what they are thinking toward.

This is where the trap begins.

Without purpose, clarity has no direction. It sharpens nothing. It becomes a tool being polished endlessly without ever being used. You see your thoughts more clearly, but they don't lead anywhere. You understand your patterns, but the patterns continue. You have insight without movement.

This is not clarity. This is observation without destination.

And observation without destination becomes overthinking.

Overthinking is not a lack of clarity. It is clarity without purpose. It is the mind trying to solve a problem it was never designed to solve: what to do when there is no clear reason to do anything.

The mind can process. It can analyse. It can weigh options, predict outcomes, rehearse scenarios. But it cannot manufacture meaning. It cannot create purpose. It can only work with what is given to it.

When nothing is given, it loops.

This is why people who think the clearest often struggle the most. They see their options with perfect precision. They understand their emotions with sharp accuracy. They know exactly what is happening inside them. And still, they cannot move.

Because seeing clearly does not tell you where to go. It only shows you where you are.

Purpose is what tells you where to go.

But purpose is not a goal. It is not an outcome. It is not something you achieve and then possess. Purpose is orientation. It is the direction your energy moves when it is not being forced.

Most people mistake purpose for ambition. They think purpose sounds like "I want to build a company" or "I want to help people" or "I want to be successful." These are goals. They are external. They can be reached, failed, or abandoned.

Purpose is internal. It does not change when circumstances do. It is not dependent on achievement or recognition. It does not require permission or validation.

Purpose is what you return to when everything else is stripped away. It is the thing that pulls your attention without effort. The work you do when no one is watching. The questions you ask when no one is grading the answers.

It is not loud. It does not announce itself. It shows up as preference. As instinct. As the quiet insistence that certain things matter more than others, even when you cannot explain why.

And when purpose is clear, personality forms naturally.

Personality is not who you perform. It is not the version of yourself you present to be liked, respected, or understood. Personality is the shape your energy takes when it is aligned with purpose.

When you know what matters, decisions simplify. Reactions become consistent. You stop shifting based on who is in the room or what is expected. Not because you are rigid, but because you are coherent.

This coherence is what people mistake for confidence. But it is not confidence in the outcome. It is confidence in the direction. You may not know if it will work. You may not know if people will approve. But you know it is yours.

That knowing is personality. Not constructed. Not curated. Just expressed.

And when personality is clear, clarity of thought follows automatically.

Because now the mind has something to work with. It is no longer trying to solve the impossible question of "what should I do with my life?" It is answering smaller, specific questions: "Does this align with what matters to me?" "Does this move me closer to where I am already going?" "Is this mine, or am I borrowing it?"

These questions have answers. They can be thought through. They do not loop endlessly because they are grounded in something real.

This is clarity. Not the ability to see every option. The ability to see which options are relevant.

And when clarity is grounded in purpose and personality, overthinking dies.

Thinking becomes functional again. It serves movement instead of replacing it.. It serves movement instead of replacing it. It processes information instead of generating anxiety. It helps you navigate instead of keeping you stuck.

Overthinking only survives in the absence of direction. When there is nowhere to go, every thought becomes a potential path. Every option feels equally valid and equally meaningless. The mind keeps searching for the "right" answer, but there is no right answer when the question itself is unclear.

Purpose clarifies the question. Personality filters the noise. Clarity executes the answer.

This is the order. And the order matters.

Most people reverse it. They try to think their way into clarity first, hoping clarity will reveal their purpose. But clarity without purpose is just sharper confusion. You see everything more vividly, but nothing stands out as mattering more than anything else.

Or they try to build a personality first, adopting traits they admire, performing the version of themselves they think they should be. But personality without purpose is just performance. It exhausts you because it requires constant maintenance. It never settles because it was never real.

Purpose must come first. Not as a grand declaration. Not as a mission statement. Just as honest acknowledgment of what pulls you without force.

You do not need to name it. You do not need to defend it. You only need to stop ignoring it.

When you stop ignoring it, something shifts. The things that felt important because everyone said they were important begin to lose weight. The things you were doing out of obligation start to feel unnecessary. The noise that was filling your mind begins to quiet, not because you silenced it, but because it was never yours to begin with.

What remains is smaller. Simpler. But it feels heavier. More real.

This is purpose asserting itself. Not as ambition. As alignment.

And once alignment exists, personality is no longer something you build. It is something you allow. You stop asking "who should I be?" and start noticing "who am I when I am not performing?"

The answer is already there. It has always been there. You just kept layering other people's expectations over it until it became invisible.

Clarity is what happens when you remove the layers. When you stop trying to think correctly and start thinking honestly. When you stop analysing every option and start moving toward what already matters.

This does not make life easier. It makes it lighter. Because you are no longer carrying the weight of everyone else's definitions, everyone else's timelines, everyone else's approval.

You are carrying your own. And your own, when it is actually yours, is always lighter than what you borrowed.

Overthinking dies here. Not because you mastered your mind. But because your mind finally has something real to work with.

It is no longer spinning in the abstract, trying to solve unsolvable questions. It is grounded. Oriented. Moving.

And movement, even slow movement, is the opposite of overthinking.

Most people never reach this point because they start in the wrong place. They start with "how do I stop overthinking?" when the real question is "what am I overthinking in service of?"

If the answer is nothing, if there is no purpose underneath the thinking, then the thinking will continue. It has to. Because the mind cannot rest in a vacuum. It will keep searching, analysing, rehearsing, preparing—not because it is broken, but because it has nothing to anchor to.

Purpose is the anchor. Personality is the current. Clarity is the surface.

You cannot fix the surface without addressing what is underneath.

So stop trying to think better. Start asking what your thinking is supposed to serve.

Not what it should serve. Not what others say it should serve. What it already serves when you are honest about where your attention naturally goes.

That is where purpose lives. Quiet. Unglamorous. Consistent.

And when you build from there, overthinking does not need to be defeated. It simply runs out of room.

Because the mind, when it has direction, does not spiral. It moves.

And movement is the only thing that has ever mattered.

You can't think your way to clarity.

You have to know what you're thinking toward first.

You can't think your way out of a directionless life.

-Be More Human-

You Are Making It Louder Than It Is.

Most problems do not arrive as disasters but as small, specific moments that appear inside an otherwise ordinary day, an email you did not expect, a conversation that shifted tone without warning, a mistake that created discomfort but not collapse. In their original form, these moments are limited. They exist in one place, at one time, with clear edges. If they were allowed to pass as they are, they would take up only as much space as they deserve.

What usually makes them feel overwhelming is not what happened, but what begins afterward.

The mind does not allow events to end cleanly. It returns to them, not to understand but to revisit, replaying details, rearranging words, imagining alternate outcomes, attaching meaning that was never present in the moment itself. What began as an event becomes a narrative, and that narrative slowly stretches beyond its original boundaries, touching parts of life it was never connected to. An issue that belonged to one hour begins to influence the entire day. Something that happened once starts to feel permanent.

This is not because the problem grew.
It is because attention did.

The mind fills uncertainty quickly. When something remains unresolved, it rushes to complete the picture, often choosing the most threatening version because uncertainty feels more dangerous than fear. Outcomes are predicted before evidence appears. Motives are assumed without confirmation. The imagination moves faster than reality ever could, and because it moves without resistance, it creates pressure that feels immediate and real.

Soon, the original situation becomes difficult to locate. It is buried under interpretation, judgment, and self-interrogation. The problem itself remains small, but the noise around it expands until it fills the entire mental space.

Most people believe this constant thinking is a form of responsibility. They confuse tension with care. Staying alert feels like staying involved, and relaxing feels like negligence. There is an unspoken belief that if the mind is not actively worrying, something important is being ignored. But much of this mental activity is not problem-solving. It is repetition. The same thoughts cycling without producing clarity, the same imagined conversations replayed without resolution.

Nothing new is being discovered.
Nothing is being repaired.

The body does not recognize this difference. It responds to repetition the same way it responds to danger. Muscles tighten. Breathing shortens. Attention narrows. The system stays active even when there is nothing to respond to. Over time, this constant alertness becomes exhausting, not because life is demanding more, but because the body never receives a signal that it can rest.

This is where many people quietly begin to shut down.

Not suddenly, and not dramatically, but gradually. Energy drops. Motivation fades. Everything feels heavier than it used to. What is later described as burnout or depression often begins here, not as sadness, but as uninterrupted pressure. The pressure to stay serious. To stay vigilant. To stay prepared for outcomes that may never arrive.

When relief does not come, the system does not rise to the challenge. It slows itself down. This is not weakness. It is survival.

Every difficulty carries two layers. The situation itself, and the meaning added to it. A missed deadline exists. The belief that it defines your competence is constructed. Financial stress is real. The conclusion that you have failed at life is imagined. Conflict happens. The story that you will always be alone is added.

The suffering rarely comes from the first layer.
It comes from the second.

These added meanings feel convincing not because they are accurate, but because they are repeated. Familiar thoughts gain authority simply by returning often. Over time, they begin to feel like facts instead of interpretations, and because they are internal, they are rarely questioned.

Control is often misunderstood at this point. People assume it means having answers, fixing things quickly, or maintaining constant composure. But control, in practice, is much smaller than that. It is the ability to notice when the mind is expanding something beyond usefulness and to choose not to follow it further. It is keeping reality in proportion instead of allowing it to turn into a verdict on your entire life.

This does not mean ignoring problems or pretending they do not matter. It means allowing them to remain specific. Contained. Touching only what they actually touch.

Action has a grounding effect that thinking does not. A message sent. A conversation started. A boundary acknowledged. When action happens, the problem returns to its actual size. It becomes something that exists in the real world again, with edges and limits. Reality is ordinary, but that ordinariness is what makes it manageable.

The mind resists this because imagination feels powerful. Reality feels slow. But imagined catastrophes do not have boundaries, while real situations do. And boundaries make things survivable.

Life rarely asks for complete clarity or total resolution. Most days ask for one honest step taken without turning it into a statement about who you are. One response instead of endless rehearsal. One decision instead of continuous anticipation.

Pausing is not avoidance.
Rest is not failure.
Silence is not surrender.

When mental noise softens, capability returns naturally. Decisions feel simpler. Attention widens again. The body relaxes not because everything is solved, but because it is no longer being asked to stay on guard indefinitely.

Problems do not usually destroy people.

Uninterrupted mental pressure does.

And when that pressure eases, life becomes workable again, not perfect and not effortless, but steady enough to move through. In that steadiness, things begin to feel human again, not because the world changed, but because the noise finally quieted enough for reality to be felt as it is.

The problem didn't grow
the noise around it did.

-Be More Human-

Your Work Doesn't Need Applause

Somewhere along the way, effort became something that needed a witness. Not just to exist, but to feel complete. The idea settled quietly, almost invisibly, that if you build something, you must also ensure it is seen, received, reacted to. As if the act itself remains unfinished until it is mirrored back by others. At first this expectation feels optional, almost harmless. Over time, it hardens into a rule.

Creation is no longer allowed to stand on its own.

It must be accompanied by acknowledgment, framed by explanation, followed by approval. Without that sequence, it feels incomplete, even when nothing is missing. The work may be done, the intention fulfilled, the effort honest, yet a subtle discomfort remains. Something feels unresolved, not because the work lacks substance, but because it has not been reflected back.

This shift changes the internal relationship with effort itself. What once felt grounded begins to feel provisional. The value of what you do starts to depend on timing, reception, and visibility. Satisfaction becomes conditional. It no longer settles on its own. It waits.

The more attention effort demands, the less solid it feels when attention arrives. Appreciation chased rarely lands cleanly. It comes with conditions, with delays, with the unspoken awareness that it could just as easily have gone elsewhere. What was once desired begins to feel thin, almost weightless. The response is there, but it does not anchor. It flickers and disappears, leaving behind the need for the next reaction.

This is not because appreciation lacks value, but because dependence erodes its weight.

In contrast, there is a quieter, sturdier freedom in doing things without arranging an audience. When work is honest, it does not require accompaniment. It does not need its maker standing beside it, translating its value, defending its existence, or insisting on its relevance. It simply exists, complete in itself.

Real work carries its own gravity.

Not the kind that pulls attention immediately, but the kind that holds shape over time. It moves slowly. It reaches people without announcement or urgency, often long after the moment of creation has passed. Sometimes it finds an audience the creator never anticipated. Sometimes it does not find one at all.

And still, it remains intact.

It's worth does not evaporate in the absence of applause. It does not become smaller because it was not celebrated. It stays whole because it was never built for reaction in the first place. Its value is not borrowed from response. It is inherent in the act of making it honestly.

The moment admiration becomes the goal, creation subtly shifts. The intent bends. The edges soften. Certain parts are emphasized while others are quietly removed. Truth becomes secondary to reception.

What began as expression starts behaving like performance.

Depth is adjusted for accessibility.
Complexity is traded for clarity that pleases.

Over time, the work stops pointing inward and starts scanning outward, measuring itself against expectation. Noise replaces substance, not suddenly, but gradually, until the exchange barely registers as meaningful. The creator is busy. The output is constant. And yet something essential feels absent.

This pursuit of validation is not accidental. It is taught early and reinforced often. Achievement is praised when it is visible. Effort is encouraged when it produces results that can be displayed. Silence is rarely rewarded. Consistency without spectacle goes unnoticed. The lesson is subtle but persistent: what matters most is not what you do, but how it appears.

What is not taught with the same consistency is how to offer recognition.

While people are encouraged to seek appreciation for themselves, they are rarely encouraged to give it freely to others. As a result, most people move through life unseen. Not invisible, but unacknowledged. Their presence is registered. Their roles are noted. Their output is consumed. But their effort is rarely recognized as effort.

They are building, maintaining, enduring, often in silence. And no one tells them it was noticed.

There is a difference between noticing someone and seeing them. Noticing is passive. It happens automatically. Seeing requires attention. It asks for presence without agenda. It does not evaluate usefulness or extract value. It simply recognizes what is already there.

Appreciation, when offered without calculation, carries a rare steadiness. It does not inflate or elevate. It does not create hierarchy. It grounds. It tells someone their effort reached something real, that it landed somewhere beyond themselves. Not as praise, but as acknowledgment.

In a world crowded with feedback loops designed to extract reaction, this kind of recognition feels almost unfamiliar. It does not demand reciprocity. It does not seek to position the giver above the receiver. It does not ask to be remembered. It simply affirms what already exists.

Being the first to recognize someone's sincerity, the first to acknowledge their consistency, the first to appreciate their presence without waiting for proof of success, is a quiet form of leadership. Not the kind built on authority or recognition, but on awareness.

It requires restraint, because it does not turn into spectacle. It requires strength, because it does not depend on being seen in return.

There is no performance in it.
Only attention.

Interestingly, those who step away from the pursuit of validation often become the ones others are drawn to. They're no longer shaped by attention. That's what makes them magnetic.

Their work feels settled. Their presence feels unhurried. There is no negotiation happening in public.

They create without desperation and appreciate without strategy.

There is a calm consistency in them, a sense that they are not asking to be confirmed. They are not waiting for permission to exist as they are. This steadiness becomes noticeable precisely because it is not trying to be. In a culture trained to amplify, restraint stands out.

The balance, when it appears, is simple but not easy.

Work done without the need for witnesses.
People seen without the need for return.
Effort offered fully.
Appreciation given freely.

No performance on either side.

In that space, creation remains honest, and recognition remains human. Integrity stays intact as a way of moving through the world without constantly asking to be affirmed.

Not because affirmation is wrong, but because it is no longer required for effort to feel complete.

Some things are complete even if no one notices.

-Be More Human-

Reflections Turned Against

Humans were never meant to see themselves this clearly.

For most of our existence, reflection was not guaranteed. You did not wake up and meet yourself. You lived first. What you were doing mattered more than how it appeared. If reflection came at all, it arrived briefly, almost by accident, and never stayed long enough to turn into judgment. Before it could settle into meaning, it dissolved.

That absence was not ignorance.
It was protection.

Reflection once confirmed existence, not evaluation. It told you that you were here, not where you stood. It did not invite inspection. It did not wait for approval. It appeared, broke apart, and moved on, quietly insisting that you move too. You could not pause long enough to audit yourself. You could not refine, compare, or rehearse your worth. Whatever you were becoming stayed in motion.

Because nothing stayed fixed, nothing could be ranked.

You could not line yourself up against others when the surface refused to hold you. There was no stable image to polish, no outcome to freeze, no position to defend. Everyone dissolved the same way. Effort blurred. Results softened. Difference lost its sharpness. In that impermanence, no one stood above or below.

You were simply human. Temporary. Unfinished. Equal.

Something changed the moment reflection became permanent.

For the first time, the self-stopped moving. It became something you could return to. Something you could study. Not just who you were, but what you had accumulated. What you represented. How far you had gone. Identity quietly shifted away from lived experience and settled into visible markers—achievements, milestones, symbols of arrival.

With that stillness came comparison.

Not loudly. Not violently. Persistently.

You no longer saw yourself alone. You saw yourself against others. Against expectations no one openly agreed to, yet everyone silently followed. Against standards that were never announced, but always present. Reflection stopped asking whether you were living and began asking where you ranked.

This measurement did not only create insecurity.

For some, reflection produced doubt—a sense of never being enough, of always trailing something unseen. For others, it produced pride. A quiet belief of being ahead. Of having crossed lines others had not. Of deserving more space. The same mechanism that diminished one person inflated another.

The damage, however, was identical.

Low self-worth and false superiority come from the same source: measurement.

The moment reflection becomes a scoreboard, humility disappears. When worth is decided by visibility, movement stops being honest. Growth turns strategic. Effort turns curated. You are no longer becoming—you are managing how becoming looks.

What once unfolded naturally now requires constant checking.

Am I ahead.
Am I behind.
Am I seen.
Am I validated.

Even while moving, a part of you stands outside yourself, observing. Correcting. Comparing.

This is where something quietly fractures.

Once you begin seeing yourself from the outside, you never fully return. A fragment of attention remains detached, monitoring position. Either tearing yourself down or lifting yourself above others. One shrinks you. The other isolates you. Both are illusions.

Reflection did not always divide the mind this way. It did not demand explanation. It did not insist on hierarchy. Earlier, it appeared briefly and left. It allowed recognition without attachment. It acknowledged existence without freezing it. And by refusing permanence, it kept life moving.

What was lost was not humility as an idea, but humility as a condition.

The natural humility that comes from motion. From not being able to hold yourself still long enough to judge. From being required to continue rather than evaluate. When reflection becomes permanent, life pauses. Attention turns inward in a way that disconnects it from experience.

What you are doing matters less than how it appears. What you are becoming matters less than how it compares.

The self turns into something to manage instead of something to inhabit.

Over time, this feels normal. Watching yourself exist becomes second nature. Moments are filtered. Meaning is delayed. Presence thins, not through excess or cruelty, but through constant observation. You are always slightly outside yourself, checking whether what you are living is acceptable, impressive, sufficient.

The problem was never reflection itself.

It was fixation.

Reflection, when it was fleeting, did not demand belief. It did not linger long enough to harden into identity. It showed you briefly, honestly, and then erased you, leaving no choice but to continue. You were not asked to interpret yourself. You were required to live.

Perhaps the issue was never how we appear, but the moment we stopped moving to decide what it meant. The moment experience was interrupted to be measured. When living turned into judging.

Fixation traps attention. It convinces you that understanding yourself requires holding still, when in fact the opposite was once true. Understanding emerged from motion, from participation, from being unable to step far enough outside yourself to construct a narrative.

When reflection becomes permanent, humility becomes performative. You either present yourself carefully or diminish yourself convincingly. Both rely on the same belief—that you are an object to be assessed.

Earlier, humility required no effort. It was not practiced. It was enforced by impermanence. By surfaces that refused to hold you. By images that would not stay. You could see yourself, but only briefly. And because you could not keep the image, you could not build a hierarchy around it.

You were required to move on.

Maybe humility was never taught through philosophy or discipline. Maybe it was learned through disappearance. Through reflections that would not stay long enough to be believed. Back when seeing yourself did not mean defining yourself. Back when looking was naturally followed by walking away.

You were never meant to be studied.
You were meant to be lived.

Life changed when you started watching yourself too closely

-Be More Human-

Content Or Narrative

People often underestimate the impact of what they consume. A video playing in the background. A headline skimmed without pause. A reel, a joke, something shared casually and forgotten just as quickly. It all feels temporary. Harmless. As if it passes through the mind without leaving a trace.

But content is never just content.

Every piece carries a direction. A tone. A way of arranging the world. Not always deliberately, not always maliciously, but inevitably. Something is always being framed. Something is always being suggested. Even when nothing is stated outright, a perspective is quietly forming.

The mind does not interact with information the way it is often assumed to. It does not wait for logic. It does not ask permission. It does not pause to verify intent. It absorbs through repetition, through emotional charge, through familiarity. What appears often enough begins to feel normal, even when it has never been examined.

What you expose yourself to consistently does not stay on the surface.

It settles. Quietly. Rearranging perception without announcement. Expectations shift. Reactions change. The transformation is rarely felt while it is happening. It is noticed later, when thoughts feel different, when emotional responses arrive faster than understanding, when restlessness appears without a clear source.

This is how narratives work.
They do not debate you.
They do not persuade you.
They normalize themselves.

An idea repeated often enough stops feeling like an opinion and starts feeling like reality. A steady stream of outrage conditions the nervous system to treat tension as a baseline. Comparison, when encountered repeatedly, creates dissatisfaction without ever naming itself as the cause. Even optimism, when manufactured and enforced, becomes another quiet pressure—another standard you feel you are failing to meet.

Over time, the voice in your head becomes less your own and more an echo of what you've absorbed.

Not because of carelessness.
Not because of weakness.

But because this is how the human mind functions.

The subconscious does not learn through reasoning. It learns through exposure. Through patterns. Through emotional repetition. Knowing better is rarely enough. The mind believes what it encounters often, not what it is told once.

This is why mindfulness matters—not as an aesthetic, not as a trend, but as awareness.

Awareness of patterns.
Awareness of emotional residue.
Awareness of what remains after the screen goes dark.

Not control. Not censorship. Just noticing. What mood does this leave behind? What assumptions does it quietly reinforce? What version of the self does it encourage without ever announcing itself?

Modern content is designed to pull attention somewhere.

Toward fear. Toward desire.
Toward outrage. Toward validation.
Toward numbness.

Engagement is the goal, not clarity. Attention is the currency, not truth.

When this goes unnoticed, emotions that were never chosen begin to feel personal. Reactions replace decisions.

A low-grade restlessness settles in. The mind stays occupied, but not clear. Something feels off, yet nothing specific can be named.

Being careful about what you consume is not about isolation or paranoia. It is about responsibility. The same responsibility already applied elsewhere. You notice what food leaves you sluggish. You avoid what makes you dependent. You understand that intake shape's function.

Content deserves the same respect.
Some of it sharpens perception. Some of it dulls it.
Some of it quietly reshapes you into someone you never consciously chose to become.

The real danger isn't negative content. It's unexamined content.

The kind absorbed daily without noticing its cumulative weight. Once awareness enters the picture, something shifts. Scrolling slows. Disengagement happens earlier. Not every emotion offered is accepted.

Distance returns, and with it, clarity.

The world does not get quieter.
You simply stop letting every noise move you.

Be careful what you consume.
Not because the world is evil,
but because the mind is porous.
And what enters it steadily, repeatedly shapes it,
whether attention is paid or not.

What you see every day slowly becomes how you think.

-Be More Human-

LOG OFF!

Somewhere along the way, anxiety stopped being a signal and started being an aesthetic. It entered language casually, folded into jokes and captions, worn lightly enough to pass as personality. "I don't think I'm okay, but I don't have time to not be okay." "I'm exhausted and I don't know from what." "Why does everything feel heavy for no clear reason?" These phrases are said without pause now, as if naming the feeling is enough to neutralise it. As if restlessness is just the texture of modern life, not something asking to be understood.

But much of what is called anxiety today does not originate where it is felt.

It arrives from the outside. Refreshed, updated, reintroduced every few seconds. Opinions layered on opinions. Emotions stacked without resolution. Events delivered without context and urgency applied without reason. The internal state begins to react to a world that never stops speaking.

You're not anxious. You're overexposed.

The human mind was never built to process hundreds of perspectives before breakfast. To compare a private life with curated fragments of strangers. To move from tragedy to trend to outrage to humour in under a minute and remain steady. Yet this has become the default rhythm. Every empty moment filled. Every pause interrupted. And then, when the noise finally stops, the silence feels unfamiliar. Almost threatening.

Not because silence is dangerous, but because it has become rare.

The nervous system does not understand notifications. It does not recognise feeds or timelines or updates. It understands stimulation. Alert. Threat. Urgency. When something lights up constantly, the body stays prepared. Not because something is happening, but because something *might*. And "might" is enough to keep the system awake.

Not because something is wrong but
because something could be.

Boredom has been replaced with scrolling. Depth with updates. The moment attention slows; the hand reaches for the screen automatically. Not to learn. Not to connect. Just to avoid the quiet. The discomfort that surfaces when nothing is being consumed is quickly labelled anxiety, instead of being recognised for what it is.

The unfamiliar feeling of being alone with your own mind.

Constant connection fragments attention. You are never fully present, never fully absent. Always responding, rarely absorbing. Always consuming, rarely integrating. Information keeps arriving, but nothing is allowed to settle. Over time, this creates a kind of exhaustion that sleep does not touch. Not physical tiredness, but mental saturation.

The mind needs space.
Not productivity.
Not stimulation.

Space.

Space to finish a thought. Space to let emotion pass without commentary. Space to connect one experience to another. Without that space, everything stays raw. Unprocessed. Loud.

The internet does not allow this kind of breathing. It rewards urgency. Outrage travels faster than calm. Extremes rise; nuance sinks. When you remain inside that environment long enough, the inner world begins to resemble it. Scattered. Reactive. Tense. Always alert, rarely at ease.

So no, nothing is wrong with you.

You are not broken.
You are not weak.
You do not need another routine to optimise yourself. What you are experiencing makes sense inside the conditions you are immersed in.

Logging off is often misunderstood as escape. As avoidance. As withdrawal from reality. But for many, it is the first return to it. When the input slows, something subtle begins to happen. Thoughts lose their edge.

Emotions settle without explanation. The background pressure eases.

Not dramatically.
Not instantly.
But enough.

Enough to remember what baseline feels like. Enough to notice how much tension was never yours to begin with. Enough to realise that clarity does not come from consuming more explanations about the mind, but from giving the mind fewer demands.

Clarity comes from allowing a thought to end. From letting boredom do what it has always done reset the system. From silence stretching long enough to stop feeling like a threat.

Anxiety is not always a personal flaw.
Sometimes, it is an environmental response.

And before diagnosing yourself, before romanticising restlessness, before turning discomfort into identity, there is a quieter possibility worth noticing.

Put the phone down.
Let the input stop.
Let the silence stretch.

Not to fix yourself.
But to remember that nothing was wrong with
you to begin with.

Your mind just needed fewer voices in it.

-Be More Human-

The Blindfold We Never Take Off

There is a quiet arrogance in the way justice is spoken about. Not loud or aggressive, but assured. As if knowing what is right or wrong were a stable position rather than a temporary one. As if clarity were something humans arrive at, instead of something they approximate. Judgments are delivered with confidence, opinions hardened into statements, conclusions announced as if the full picture were ever visible.

But it never is.

Every judgment rests on fragments. On partial accounts passed through biased mouths. On memories softened or sharpened by time. On narratives shaped less by fact and more by feeling. What is seen is always incomplete. What is known is always interrupted. There are moments that never reach awareness, decisions made under pressures that remain invisible, timelines that never cross the observer's path.

No story arrives whole.

People carry histories that do not announce themselves. Motives layered over wounds. Scars buried so deeply that even the person carrying them forgets where they began. Actions that look deliberate from the outside are often responses formed long before the moment they are judged. Causes are mistaken for intentions. Outcomes are confused with character.

So how could justice, in any human sense, be pure?

It cannot be. Not because humans are cruel, but because humans are limited. Perception itself is filtered. By experience. By pain. By loyalty. By moral codes inherited rather than chosen. Justice cannot be objective when the observer never is. The lens shapes the verdict before the facts ever arrive.

In one timeline, a choice is made out of love. In another, the same choice destroys someone's life.

In a third, neither version exists because something entirely different unfolded.

Yet the judgment remains confident.

Certainty is comforting. Sides are easier than complexity. Heroes and villains simplify what is otherwise exhausting to hold. Neutrality feels like indecision. Doubt is mistaken for weakness. So, lines are drawn quickly. Positions taken firmly. Context discarded quietly.

But truth does not live cleanly inside one version of events.

It exists in overlap. In contradiction. In the invisible spaces where perspectives collide and dissolve each other. Where intent and impact refuse to align neatly. Where no single account survives without losing something essential.

Justice, if it exists at all, may not be about deciding who was right.

It may be about understanding why things fractured the way they did.

That understanding is slower. Less satisfying. It offers no clear winner. It does not reward outrage or loyalty. It asks for patience in a culture that values speed. It requires sitting with uncertainty without trying to resolve it immediately.

Before speaking of justice, there is always a pause available.

Before declaring who deserved what, there is always a missing thread. A version never heard. A moment that changes the shape of everything that follows. This absence is not an exception. It is the rule.

There is always a story you did not see.

The blindfold is not something worn deliberately. It is built into perception itself. No amount of conviction removes it. No strength of opinion dissolves it. Everyone looks from somewhere. Everyone sees partially. Everyone judges with limits they cannot fully step outside of.

Wisdom, then, is not found in confident verdicts.

It is found in restraint.

In recognising how little is actually known. In resisting the urge to reduce human lives to conclusions. In choosing empathy not as virtue, but as acknowledgment of uncertainty. In understanding that certainty often says more about the observer than the truth being observed.

In a world constructed from incomplete truths, the quietest strength is not judgment.

It is awareness.

No one ever sees the full story.

-Be More Human-

ACT II
(Learning to stand)

Trees

Everything today wants to be fast. Growth is expected to announce itself. Progress is judged by how quickly it can be displayed. Careers, relationships, healing, confidence—each is pushed into timelines that ignore how humans actually form. Movement is demanded even when nothing inside is ready to support it.

So, people rush.

They move forward before they understand what they are building toward. They accept responsibility before developing the strength to carry it. They seek connection before learning how to remain emotionally present. On the surface, this looks like ambition. Underneath, it often feels like instability.

That instability does not always arrive loudly.

Most of the time, it shows up quietly.

A career that keeps advancing but feels hollow. A relationship that begins intensely and fractures under ordinary pressure. Confidence that sounds convincing until it is questioned. Life appears full, impressive, busy—yet something feels misaligned. The pace is high, but the footing feels uncertain.

The issue is not effort.

It is foundation.

Foundations are invisible. No one applauds emotional regulation, patience, self-awareness, consistency. These qualities do not photograph well. They do not produce immediate validation. In a world built around visibility, they are dismissed as delays rather than necessities.

But they are not optional.

Without them, growth becomes fragile. Without them, success requires constant reinforcement. Without them, even small disruptions feel overwhelming. The structure looks tall, but it cannot hold weight.

Outside this urgency—beyond timelines, comparisons, and noise—something else has been growing quietly, without concern for recognition.

Trees do not announce progress.

They do not mark milestones.
They do not perform growth.

For years, sometimes decades, their most important work happens underground. Before height, before branches, before shade, there is anchoring. Roots spreading slowly. Learning the soil. Adjusting to resistance. Finding stability where no one is watching.

This is not hesitation.

It is intelligence.

A tree does not rush upward because height means nothing without support. It understands, instinctively, that expansion without grounding leads to collapse. Stability is built first. Growth follows only when it can be sustained.

That single principle explains their calm.

Storms come. Winds shift. Seasons change. Still, they remain. Not because they are untouched by force, but because they are prepared for it. Strong roots do not prevent storms.

They make survival possible.

Humans are no different.

Skills without fundamentals fail under pressure. Confidence without self-knowledge becomes defensive. Ambition without values turns restless. Emotional openness without boundaries leads to exhaustion. What appears strong from the outside is often speed mistaken for depth.

Trees do not grow by comparison.

One does not rush because another grew taller faster. They do not twist themselves to meet the expectations of the forest. Each grows according to what its roots can support, not what the environment demands it display.

That patience is not weakness.
It is self-respect.

There is another lesson trees offer, quieter but just as important how they give.

They offer shade without deciding who deserves it. They release oxygen without expectation. They bear fruit without announcing effort. Giving is not a strategy for them.

It is a consequence of health.
This distinction matters more than it seems.

When humans give without grounding, it drains them. When they support others without boundaries, resentment builds. When they show up without inner stability, burnout follows. Giving becomes transactional, conditional, or performative.

Trees give because they can.

Not because they are trying to prove anything.

A grounded human gives the same way. Not constantly. Not loudly. Not at the cost of themselves. Their presence steadies' others simply because they are steady. Their generosity does not feel forced because it is not compensating for inner lack.

This is what depth creates.

Depth takes time. It requires sitting with discomfort instead of escaping it. Learning without immediate reward. Developing discipline when no one is watching. Understanding oneself without external affirmation. These processes are slow, and they rarely look impressive while they are happening.

That is why they are often skipped.

Roots grow in silence.

And silence is uncomfortable.

But silence is also where structure forms.

Trees do not chase visibility. They do not apologise for growing slowly. They do not panic when progress is unseen. They trust the process they are built for.

Humans often do the opposite.

Speed becomes proof of worth. Stillness is mistaken for stagnation. Quiet growth is interpreted as falling behind. Yet many times, what appears stagnant is actually preparation.

The world rewards what can be displayed.

Life rewards what can endure.

When fundamentals are strong emotional awareness, patience, discipline, clarity growth does not need constant defence. It does not shatter at the first sign of pressure. It does not feel like something that must be protected at all costs.

It simply stands.

This does not mean rejecting ambition or connection.

It means earning them.

Allowing growth to rise from depth instead of using growth to conceal the absence of it.

Trees remind us that becoming solid matters more than becoming impressive.

That stability comes before expansion. That giving is sustainable only when it flows from strength.

In a world obsessed with speed, choosing depth is a quiet rebellion.

Build what cannot be seen.
Strengthen what cannot be shown.
Let growth arrive when it can stay.

That is when progress stops feeling fragile.
That is when giving stops feeling draining.
That is when growth becomes real.

And that is where you become more human.

Real strength grows where no one is looking.

-Be More Human-

Do Something
That Makes You Feel Real

There is a reason people feel more alive when they are tired from doing something that mattered. Not exhausted in a numb, depleted way, but used. The body recognises the difference immediately. One kind of tiredness empties you out. The other settles you into yourself. Sleep comes easier. Breath feels deeper. Presence feels heavier.

The body knows when it has been involved.

There is a particular clarity that follows effort. Not excitement. Not pride. Just a grounded sense of having occupied your own life instead of hovering around it. The fatigue carries meaning. It does not demand escape. It feels earned.

Effort, in its simplest form, is not about chasing a future. It is about staying with the present long enough to shape it. Returning to the same place, the same task, the same responsibility, even after novelty has worn off and nothing about it feels impressive.

When you keep showing up—especially when it is boring, especially when no one is watching—something inside begins to settle.

You stop floating.
You start standing somewhere.

Floating feels light, but it is unstable. Days blur together. Time passes without resistance.

Everything is consumed; nothing is held. Effortless living often looks peaceful from the outside, but inside it carries drift.

No friction. No anchor. No sense of being needed by anything.

Standing somewhere creates weight. It creates location. You are not everywhere, but you are *here*. And that "here" begins to matter.

Most days do not feel important. They feel ordinary. A desk. A road. A task already done before. There is no ceremony around them. No sense of arrival. Just repetition. But when you give yourself to those repetitions—when you stay instead of escaping, they begin to give something back.

Not immediately.
Not dramatically.

Slowly.

You gain weight. Not physical weight, but inner weight. The kind that steadies reactions. The kind that allows silence without discomfort. The kind that makes you harder to shake. This weight does not announce itself. It does not need language. It shows up in posture. In patience. In how you move through a day.

The universe does not respond to intention.

It responds to contact.

To hands that keep touching the work. To minds that return to the same problem even after the feeling has changed. To people who do not disappear the moment motivation fades. Consistency creates a relationship with reality that intention alone never can.

There is a quiet warmth in effort. Even when uncomfortable, it keeps you awake inside your own life. You are not watching time pass. You are participating in it. The day presses back against you, and you respond. That exchange creates texture.

This is what makes a day feel lived instead of merely survived.

Without effort, time becomes something that happens *to* you. With effort, time becomes something you move *through*. The difference is subtle, but cumulative. Weeks shaped by engagement feel dense. Weeks without it feel thin, even when busy.

People who avoid effort often say they want peace. What they usually encounter is dullness. Nothing challenges them. Nothing resists them. And because nothing pushes back, nothing pushes them inward either. They remain unshaped. Restless. Under stimulated at a deeper level.

Resistance is what gives form.

You begin to feel human when something resists you. When a day asks something from you. When energy must be summoned rather than spent. When you have to lean in instead of scrolling past. When you are required to show up with your body, your attention, your patience.

Consumption cannot do this.

Consumption fills time, but it does not anchor it. It occupies the senses without engaging the self. You can consume endlessly and still feel untouched by the day. Engagement leaves marks. Even small engagement. Especially small engagement, repeated.

Effort is not about greatness.
It is not about success.

It is about presence.

Presence is not a mood. It is not something you think yourself into. It arrives when attention is fully involved. When hands are busy. When the mind is occupied by something that exists outside itself. Presence happens when there is something to respond to.

This is why effort brings people back into their bodies.

Breath becomes noticeable. Time stretches or compresses. Limits are felt. You are no longer just thinking about life—you are *inside* it. Even fatigue feels cleaner when it comes from use rather than avoidance.

There is dignity in work that does not ask to be seen. In consistency that never becomes content. In effort that builds something quiet and durable inside a person. Over time, it builds trust with oneself.

You begin to believe yourself.

Not because you achieved something extraordinary, but because you stayed. Because you returned. Because you did not vanish when motivation left. That trust becomes grounding. Something external praise cannot replace.

Effort anchor's identity in action rather than image. You stop asking who you are and start experiencing it. Not as a story, but as rhythm. The rhythm of showing up. Of engaging with something real.

This is why demanding work can feel calming. The mind has less room to spiral when it is occupied by reality. Anxiety thrives in abstraction. Presence grows in contact.

When effort disappears, abstraction takes over. Thoughts multiply. Energy scatters. The body remains idle while the mind races. Nothing feels urgent enough to alarm you, but nothing feels solid either.

Engagement corrects this imbalance.

Not through force.
Through involvement.

It reunites thinking with doing. This is why clarity often follows physical or focused work, even when the work itself was not enjoyable. Something real was encountered. Something required response.

That response makes you feel real in return.

Effort does not promise happiness. It does not guarantee fulfilment. What it offers is simpler and more fundamental—a sense of inhabiting your own life. Of being located somewhere rather than drifting through days.

You feel the ground under your feet.

That grounding does not come from comfort. It comes from contribution. From friction. From being required. From knowing that something would not exist in the same way if you did not show up.

This is why effortless days fade, while difficult days remain. The memory is not of strain, but of participation. Of being pulled into the day rather than passing through it untouched.

Effort does not make life easier.
It makes it *real*.

And reality, even when demanding, stabilises. It gives shape to time. It gives weight to identity. It gives the nervous system something honest to respond to.

This is not about glorifying struggle.

It is about recognising that avoidance does not bring peace. It brings disconnection.

A life without effort becomes soft in ways that make it fragile.

A life with effort becomes sturdy, even when imperfect.

Presence is not found by turning inward endlessly.

It is found by meeting the world where it resists you.

By doing something.
By staying it.
By letting effort place you back inside your own life.

That is what real work gives.

Not greatness.
Not success.
But presence.

You felt alive because you were actually there.

-Be More Human"

Grinding For the Wrong Life

Most people do not choose their purpose. They inherit it.

It arrives quietly, without ceremony. From family expectations. From cultural definitions of success. From what appears respectable, impressive, or secure. No one hands it to you all at once. It comes in pieces. A suggestion here. An approval there. A warning about what not to be. Over time, those fragments assemble themselves into a direction you begin to follow without ever consciously deciding to.

Eventually, you find yourself chasing a life that never really belonged to you.

The problem is not ambition.

The problem is borrowed ambition.

Borrowed ambition looks identical to the real thing from the outside. It demands discipline. It requires sacrifice. It consumes time, energy, and attention. You grind just as hard. Sometimes harder. Because when the drive does not come from within, effort has to compensate. Motivation becomes something you manufacture instead of something you return to naturally.

And when you work toward something that is not yours, it still asks for everything.

Your mornings.
Your patience.
Your best years.

You show up. You perform. You progress. But there is a subtle disconnect running underneath it all. The work never fully lands inside you. It never settles. It feels like movement without arrival. Activity without ownership.

When it does not work out, the damage goes deeper than disappointment.

You do not just lose the outcome.
You lose your sense of self.

Because when the goal was never truly yours, failure does not feel like information. It feels like exposure. You begin to think *you* are the problem. That you lacked discipline. That you were not strong enough. That you wasted time. In reality, you were simply running in the wrong direction.

There is a specific kind of exhaustion that comes from building a life you cannot feel inside.

You can be productive and still feel empty. You can be praised and still feel misplaced. You can hit milestones and still feel strangely detached from them. On paper, everything looks correct. In conversation, it sounds impressive. Yet something refuses to settle.

Because somewhere beneath the effort, a quieter awareness persists.

You are performing someone else's idea of success.

This kind of exhaustion is not relieved by rest. Time off helps the body, but it does not touch the misalignment. Even breaks begin to feel strange, because returning to the work feels heavier than it should. The mind resists not because the work is difficult, but because it feels unrelated.

Society is very good at handing out templates.

Study this.
Become that.
Want these things.
Avoid those risks.

Templates are efficient. They reduce uncertainty. They offer safety in numbers. If enough people follow the same path, it begins to feel validated. But a template cannot tell you where you belong. It can only tell you where people usually go.

Belonging cannot be outsourced.

Purpose does not live on a list. It does not announce itself through titles or income brackets. It does not reveal itself through comparison. It is recognised indirectly when effort stops feeling like self-betrayal. When work, even when demanding, feels aligned rather than forced. When fatigue arrives without resentment.

This does not mean the work becomes easy.

Struggle still exists. Resistance remains.

Doubt still appears. But the struggle feels honest. It does not make you question your identity. It does not erode your sense of direction. It simply makes you tired.

And that is a very different kind of tired.

Failure also changes shape when the direction is your own.

It still hurts. Loss still stings. But it does not hollow you out. It does not shrink you. Instead of eroding your sense of self, it sharpens it. You do not come out smaller. You come out clearer. You learn. You adjust. You continue.

Failure only becomes destructive when the dream was never yours to begin with.

In that case, it teaches nothing. It just confirms a doubt you were already carrying. A quiet suspicion that something about this life never fit. Each setback reinforces the feeling of being misplaced, rather than offering insight into what went wrong.

Finding your own purpose is not about being special.

It is about being honest.

Honest about what holds your attention when nobody is watching. Honest about what you return to without external pressure. Honest about what feels meaningful even before it becomes rewarding. These signals are subtle. They are easy to dismiss because they do not arrive with urgency or validation.

Borrowed ambition is loud.
Personal direction is quiet.

One is reinforced constantly. The other requires listening.

When you begin moving in the right direction, something subtle shifts. The work still demands effort. Days are still long. Doubt still visits. But the effort no longer feels like a performance. You are no longer convincing yourself to care. You are responding to something that already matters.

The exhaustion that follows feels clean.

You know why you are tired.

There is relief in that clarity. Not comfort, but steadiness. Even difficult days feel connected to something larger than survival or approval. You stop measuring yourself constantly. You stop needing external confirmation to justify the effort.

This does not mean certainty arrives. Purpose is not a permanent state of knowing. It is not a final answer. It is a direction that continues to make sense even as conditions change. Alignment is not perfection. It is coherence.

Grinding for the wrong life fractures that coherence.

The more effort you pour in, the more distant you feel from yourself. Achievement becomes hollow. Praise feels misplaced. Rest feels undeserved. Even success carries a strange weight, because something inside knows it was achieved at the cost of authenticity.

Grinding for the right life does not eliminate hardship.

It simply ensures the hardship does not erase you.

You remain intact within the struggle. You do not disappear into the role. You do not lose your sense of agency. You feel tired, but not displaced. Challenged, but not disconnected.

Most people do not fail because they lack discipline.

They fail because they are disciplined in service of something that was never theirs.

When direction is borrowed, effort becomes a transaction. You give your time in exchange for approval, safety, or status. When direction is personal, effort becomes participation. You are building something you recognise, even if you cannot fully explain it yet.

The difference is not visible immediately.

But over time, it becomes unmistakable.

One path steadily drains you, no matter how successful it looks.
The other sustains you, even when progress is slow.

Grinding is not the problem.

Grinding for the wrong life is.

Working hard means nothing if the direction isn't yours.

-Be More Human-

Learning To Drive Yourself

People often believe life becomes easier when circumstances improve. When money settles. When people behave differently. When problems disappear. There is an assumption that ease arrives from the outside, that the road smooths out and the ride becomes comfortable.

But what actually makes life easier is quieter than that.

It is knowing what is happening inside you while everything else is happening around you.

Most people do not live from awareness. They live from momentum. A thought appears. It creates a feeling. The feeling turns into an emotion. And before there is any pause, action has already happened. Words are spoken. Reactions land. Decisions are made. Only afterward does reflection arrive.

Then comes the question.
Why did I say that.
Why did I react that way.
Why did this drain me so much.

The answer is usually simple.

Presence was missing.

You were not choosing. You were being carried.

The internal world is always in motion. Thoughts rise. Emotions shift. Impulses push forward. Habits repeat themselves. This movement is natural. The problem is not that it exists. The problem is when it runs unattended.

Your mind, emotions, impulses, and habits are powerful. They move quickly. They respond instantly. They can take you far. But power without awareness does not bring freedom.

It brings drift.

Without awareness, the system reacts to whatever appears. A message.

A tone.
A memory.

A fear that colours everything that follows.

The response feels justified and personal, but it is automatic.

This is what it means to live without a driver.

When you do not know yourself, your fears take the wheel. Your insecurities decide direction. Your moods control speed. A small comment can ruin a day. A little praise can shift your sense of self. You become easy to push and easy to pull.

Not because you are weak.
Because there is no pause.

Everything that enters you moves straight into action.

This constant reaction creates exhaustion. Not the exhaustion of effort, but the exhaustion of being moved around by your own internal machinery. Life feels chaotic even when nothing extreme is happening.

Knowing yourself does not mean suppressing anything.

It means noticing.

You begin to see anger as it rises, not after it has spoken for you. You sense fear before it tightens decisions. You feel sadness before it pulls the day inward. This noticing does not remove emotion.

It creates space.

Not a dramatic gap.
Just enough.

And inside that space, a choice appears.

You can still feel everything. But you do not have to become everything you feel.

That is what makes life smoother. Not because the road improves, but because handling improves. You stop swerving with every emotion. You stop crashing into situations you could have moved through differently.

Nothing becomes perfect. Mistakes still happen. Emotions still arrive uninvited. But awareness returns faster. Recovery shortens.

Damage does not compound as easily.

At first, awareness arrives late. Then it arrives midway. Sometimes, it arrives before action. This is not control.

It is participation.

You are present with what is happening inside you instead of being absent from it. Over time, this presence reduces chaos. Not because less goes wrong, but because less hijacks you completely.

You begin to trust yourself.

Not because you always get it right, but because you know you will notice when you don't. You know you will catch yourself before things spiral too far.

Many people try to improve life by changing environments, people, or circumstances. But without awareness, patterns repeat. The scenery changes. The reactions don't.

Learning to drive yourself does not mean the journey becomes easy.

It means the journey becomes *yours*.

Even difficult moments feel cleaner. You know what you are feeling and why. You know what belongs to the moment and what belongs to you. Pain still exists, but confusion loosens its grip.

Life feels steadier.
Not quieter.
Not slower.
Just steadier.

Life does not become easier because nothing goes wrong.

It becomes easier because you are finally there when it does.

Life felt calmer once you stopped being carried by it.

-Be More Human

The Body Remembers

The mind can accept things the body refuses.

You understand, intellectually, that you're safe. Your chest still tightens when someone raises their voice. You know a relationship ended for clear reasons. Your stomach still drops when you see their name. You've moved past something. Your breath still shortens when the memory surfaces.

The body does what it was built to do: remember.

The mind works through language, logic, narrative. It builds stories that make sense of what happened. It creates distance. It finds meaning. It moves on.

The body stores.

Every moment of fear, every instance of betrayal, every shock too fast to process consciously gets written into tissue. Into the nervous system. Into breath patterns and muscle tension and the way you hold yourself when you walk into a room.

The body remembers what the mind has forgotten. And it responds accordingly.

Anxiety arrives without reason. Certain places make you tense without conscious explanation. Some people feel safe and others don't, even when nothing obvious differs.

The body isn't confused. It's responding to information is stored. Information that bypassed thought entirely and went straight into the system that keeps you alive.

This system doesn't care about fairness or accuracy. It cares about survival. And survival, in the body's language, means: if it hurt before, avoid it now.

So the body contracts. It braces. It tightens in preparation for impact, even when no impact is coming. It treats the present like the past. A raised voice now sounds like the raised voice then. A moment of silence now feels like the silence before something terrible happened.

The body doesn't analyse. It reacts.

And it reacts faster than thought. You feel the response before you understand what triggered it. The breath shortens. The heart rate climbs. The muscles prepare to fight or flee. Only afterward does the mind arrive, trying to make sense of what the body already knows.

Philosophy alone cannot heal trauma.

You can understand what happened. You can reframe the narrative. You can reach intellectual clarity about why you react the way you do. Until the body releases what it's holding, the reaction persists.

The mind says, "That was years ago. I am safe now."

The body says, "This feeling is familiar. Prepare."
The body wins. Every time.

The body has been keeping you alive longer than your mind has been making sense of your life. It doesn't trust language. It trusts sensation. And sensation, once learned, doesn't unlearn itself just through thinking.

Real release happens in the body. Through movement. Through breath that's allowed to complete itself. Through shaking, crying, stillness, sound. Through letting the body finish what it started years ago and was never allowed to complete.

When danger appears, the body mobilizes energy. Heart rate increases. Breath quickens. Muscles flood with adrenaline. The system prepares to fight or run.

But often, neither is possible. You cannot fight. You cannot run. You freeze. You endure. You survive by shutting down.

The energy mobilized for action gets trapped. It never discharges. It stays in the system, waiting. And it waits for years, sometimes decades, creating the background tension that never fully resolves.

You can feel exhausted without doing anything. Rest doesn't restore you. Your body feels tight even when nothing is currently wrong.

The charge is still there. Still waiting for release.

Talking doesn't release it. Understanding doesn't release it. Reframing the story doesn't release it.

What releases it is allowing the body to move the way it wanted to move when the threat was present. Allowing the breath to deepen. Allowing the shaking to happen. Allowing tears that were held back. Allowing the scream that was swallowed.

The body doesn't need drama. It needs permission. Permission to finish what it started. Permission to discharge what it's been holding. Permission to update the stored information from "danger" to "past."

This process is physical. It happens in sensation, not in thought. And it requires presence, not analysis.

You don't need to understand why your chest tightens. You only need to feel it tightening, stay with it, and allow it to soften when it's ready. You don't need to know why your throat closes. You only need to breathe into it, feel the constriction, and wait for the release that comes when the body trusts it's safe to let go.

Most people abandon the process here. Sensation without narrative feels unbearable. The mind wants to explain, fix, resolve. The body just wants to feel.

But feeling is the way through.

Not thinking about the feeling. Not analysing it. Not turning it into a story. Just feeling it. Letting it be present. Letting it move. Letting it complete.

When this happens, something shifts. Not in your understanding. In your system.

The tightness loosens. The breath deepens. The body stops bracing against a threat that's no longer present. The reaction that felt automatic begins to soften.

This doesn't happen once. It happens in layers. The body releases what it's ready to release, and holds what it's not ready to release. You don't get to decide the timeline. You only get to show up and allow the process.

Over time, the body begins to trust that it's safe to let go. That the past isn't happening now. That the threat has ended. You didn't convince it with logic. You stayed present with the sensation long enough for the system to update itself.

The mind will always try to take over. To explain. To manage. To control. Let it. But don't let it distract you from what the body is saying.

The body remembers what the mind has buried. And until you allow it to speak, to move, to release, the memory stays active. Not as thought, but as tension. As reactivity. As the feeling that something is wrong even when nothing currently is.

The mind can say you are safe. But the body won't believe it until it feels safe. And it only feels safe when it's allowed to complete what was interrupted.

So, breathe. Move. Feel. Let the body finish what it started.
It's the only way the body knows how to heal.

When You Are In Control The Mind Calms

Confidence is not the belief that nothing will go wrong. It is the certainty that even if something does, you will not disappear inside it. That you will remain present. That you will respond rather than unravel.

Anxiety begins where self-trust weakens.

Not because you are incapable, and not because you lack intelligence or skill, but because the mind does not yet believe you are in control of yourself. When that trust is missing, the mind compensates. It scans. It rehearses. It anticipates danger not because danger is certain, but because uncertainty feels unmanaged.

So, it stays alert.
Tense.
Loud.

The mind is not trying to sabotage you. It is trying to protect you in the only way it knows how by staying ahead of every possible outcome. When it does not trust the one steering it, it refuses to rest.

Confidence quiets that noise.

When you trust yourself, the future stops feeling like a threat. Not because it becomes predictable, but because unpredictability no longer feels fatal. You do not need guarantees. You do not need reassurance layered on reassurance. You only need to know that when the moment arrives, you will meet it with clarity instead of panic.

Calm does not come from safety.
It comes from competence.

This is why confident people feel unhurried. They do not over-explain. They do not react to every stimulus. They are not rushing to close every open loop. Their movements are deliberate, not because they are certain of outcomes, but because they are prepared to respond.

They are not trying to outrun uncertainty.
They are willing to meet it.

Many people try to manage anxiety by controlling the external world. They plan excessively. They avoid situations that feel unstable. They seek reassurance from others. They try to arrange life so that nothing unexpected can touch them.

But control was never meant to be outsourced.

The mind relaxes only when it trusts the one guiding it. No amount of external order can compensate for internal uncertainty. Schedules help, environments matter, preparation has value—but none of it settles the nervous system if self-trust is missing.

Confidence is that trust.

It is not built through affirmations or beliefs alone. It forms through evidence. Quiet evidence. Accumulated over time.

Moments where you stayed present inside discomfort instead of escaping it. Moments where you made a decision without perfect information and survived the outcome. Moments where you recovered after mistakes instead of collapsing into self-doubt. Moments where you showed yourself that you could endure without breaking.

Each of these moments teaches the nervous system something subtle but powerful.

I am safe with me.

That belief does not arrive suddenly. It settles gradually. And when it does, anxiety loses its leverage. Not because it disappears, but because it no longer needs to shout.

This does not mean nervousness ends. It means nervousness no longer owns you. You can feel it, register it, and continue anyway. Sensation no longer equals command.

Control is not about suppressing emotion.
It is about not being ruled by it.

Real confidence is internal authority. It is knowing your values well enough to orient yourself when things feel unclear. Knowing your limits well enough to respect them without shrinking.

Knowing your direction well enough to move without constant permission.

It is the ability to pause before reacting and choose your response with intention.

That pause is not hesitation.
It is power.

Most people mistake intensity for strength and speed for control. But steadiness is quieter than that. It does not announce itself. It reveals itself over time, in consistency rather than breakthrough.

Strength grows where promises are kept. Small ones. Private ones. The kind no one applauds. Over time, those moments compound. The body softens. Thoughts lose urgency. The constant background tension fades.

Not because life becomes easier, but because you become steadier.

You do not eliminate fear.
You outgrow dependence on it.
And when the mind finally trusts the one steering it,
anxiety no longer needs to protect you.
It steps aside.

The mind relaxes when it trusts you.

-Be More Human-

What Comes Easy Still Counts

There is something you do exceptionally well, and the reason you do not recognise it as a skill is simple. It does not disturb you. It does not demand effort or create tension. It does not require preparation or recovery.

It moves through you quietly, the way something natural does.

So, you assume it is basic.
You assume it is shared.
You assume it does not count.

What feels easy is often mistaken for what is insignificant. Not because it lacks depth, but because it does not announce itself.

It does not arrive with struggle or resistance. It does not leave you depleted. It does not demand applause. It simply works.

Ease is not a lack of substance.

Some abilities do not arrive through effort. They arrive through alignment. They sit so close to who you are that separating them from yourself feels unnecessary. You do not *perform* them. You inhabit them. They are not something you switch on. They are something you move from.

That is why they feel ordinary.

You were taught to measure value through difficulty. Through strain. Through how much something costs you. If it did not exhaust you, it must not matter. If it did not hurt, it must not be serious. If it did not require sacrifice, it must be replaceable.

But this way of measuring misses something essential.

The most reliable strengths are often the quietest ones. They do not seek attention. They do not need to be defended. They stabilise situations without trying to control them. They clarify without forcing explanation. They hold things together without appearing to do much at all.

These strengths are easy to overlook because they do not ask for permission to exist.

They show up without drama.

Notice what you return to without resistance. Not what you push yourself toward, but what draws you back gently, even when no one is watching.

Notice what people trust you with, often without explaining why.

Notice where conversations soften in your presence.
Where decisions become clearer.
Where complexity reduces instead of multiplying.
Notice where things become simpler when you are involved.
These patterns are not accidents.
They are evidence.

What comes naturally to you often carries responsibility, not because it is heavy, but because it is steady.

It does not rush. It does not overcorrect.

It does not try to prove itself. It sees clearly and moves accordingly. Because it does not demand validation, you were never taught to respect it.

You learned to respect effort. You learned to admire struggle. You learned to glorify what looks difficult from the outside.

So, when something works without friction, you discount it.
You treat it as luck, or coincidence,
or something anyone could do.

But not everyone can.
Ease usually means something is already integrated.
Already absorbed.
Already aligned with your way of seeing and responding.
It does not mean it lacks value.
It means it does not fight you.
And that matters.
Growth does not always require resistance.
Sometimes it requires recognition.

Sometimes the most honest expansion comes from trusting what already holds instead of chasing what feels impressive.

If something feels easy, do not dismiss it too quickly.

Ease often means it is settled.
It means it belongs to you.
It means it has weight without noise.

You do not need to fight yourself to grow.

You do not need to manufacture difficulty to feel legitimate.
Pay attention to what remains stable when everything else feels uncertain.

Let that be enough.

Build from there.

Ease isn't accidental.
It is familiarity earned over time.

-Be More Human-

ACT III
(Relating Without Illusion)

Don't Wait to Love

Love is often mistaken for something that belongs only to romance.

It is narrowed into chemistry, attraction, moments that look good from the outside. It becomes something dramatic, something exceptional, something that requires the right conditions.

But love is far more ordinary than that, and far more essential.

It lives quietly, in places that rarely get named.

In how time is offered. In how attention is held.

In the choice to be present with people when nothing remarkable is happening.

Most love does not arrive as intensity. It does not resemble a scene or a declaration.

It looks like staying a little longer when someone is tired, even when leaving would be easier.

It looks like listening without dividing attention, without checking something else while words are being spoken. It looks like remembering a detail shared weeks ago and returning to it, not because it was important in itself, but because the person was.

Love does not need volume to be real. It needs continuity.

These gestures rarely feel significant while they are happening. They blend into the background of ordinary days.

But they do something precise. They make someone feel real to another person.

Not impressive. Not admired. Real. And that recognition carries weight long after the moment passes.

There is a quiet belief that sits beneath most postponement.

The belief that there is time.

Time to say it later.
Time to show up properly next time.
Time to be more present when life slows down.

Care is delayed as if it were endlessly repeatable. Small acts are postponed as if they carry no urgency. It feels reasonable. Responsible, even. Life is busy. Energy fluctuates. Distraction feels harmless. The assumption is that what matters can always be returned to.

But time does not move with awareness.

It does not announce itself.
It does not warn.
It does not pause for readiness.

It keeps going, indifferent to intention. What feels ordinary while it is happening does not always remain available. Moments that seemed interchangeable turn out not to be. Conversations assumed to be ongoing reach their end without signalling that they are about to do so.

This is why regret rarely centres on what was done.

It gathers around what was left undone.

The calls not made.
The words held back.
The moments when attention was elsewhere.

Days dismissed as routine that later reveal themselves as the last shared with someone. Not dramatic days. Not meaningful by design. Just days that were present once and then were not.

Regret does not announce itself loudly. It does not arrive as a breakdown.

It whispers. It appears in quiet moments, often long after the opportunity has passed.

It sounds like I should have said that.
It sounds like *why did I wait.*

It feels like remembering something clearly while knowing there is no way to return to it.

Love, in contrast, does not require preparation.

It is not something you wait to be ready for.
It is not something you save for better circumstances.

It is something you practice.

Not when days are clean and moods are settled, but in the middle of unfinished conversations and imperfect attention. It is given when energy is low. When presence costs something. When the gesture feels too small to matter. That is often when it matters most.

A simple message sent without reason.
A long hug that lingers longer than expected.
A moment of undivided attention when distraction would be easier.

These things pass without ceremony. They are rarely remembered by the one giving them. But they settle deeply in the one receiving them. Later, they become reference points. Proof that someone noticed. That someone stayed. That someone cared without being prompted.

There is a tendency to save love for a future version of yourself.

Someone with more time.
More clarity.
More emotional capacity.

That version feels responsible, capable, ready. But it does not exist. There is only the person you are now, moving through the days as they are. And the people who matter to you exist only in

Love does not need to be refined before it is given.
It does not need to be impressive.
It does not need to be perfect.

It needs to be offered while the moment is still open.

Said while it can still be heard.
Shown while it can still be felt.

Given while there is still someone there to receive it.

Waiting for the right moment often means waiting past the moment that mattered. What feels small now often becomes large later, simply because it was present when presence was possible.

Love is not measured by intensity.

It is measured by continuity.

By the willingness to show up repeatedly, without guarantee, without performance.

By choosing presence over postponement,

even when nothing seems at stake.

One day, what remains will not be the plans you had or the intentions you carried quietly.

It will be what you chose to give while you were there to give it. The time you stayed.

The attention you offered.

The care you did not delay.

That is what lasts.

You thought you had time.
That's the part that hurts later.

-Be More Human-

Moments Are Quiet Memories Are Louder

We spend most of our lives chasing outcomes.

Bigger goals.

Better versions.

Safer futures.

There is always something ahead that feels more important than what is happening now. And in that process, we quietly neglect the only thing that ever becomes real later moments.

Moments feel small while they're happening.

They don't announce themselves.

They don't demand attention.

They pass while the mind is elsewhere, already leaning into what's next.

Memories don't behave like that. Memories grow louder with time. They return when life slows down, when distractions thin out, when you finally sit still long enough to hear yourself. That's why moments are ignored.

They ask for presence now, but they offer their weight later.

When life actually slows down not during achievements, not during applause, not during milestones, but during silence something becomes clear.

You don't remember how productive you were.

You don't remember how busy your days looked or how many things you managed at once.

You remember how someone made you feel.

A laugh you didn't rush through.
A call you didn't cut short.
A conversation you stayed in, even when it was uncomfortable.

Years later, life doesn't replay events. It replays emotions.

The feeling of being understood or dismissed.

The sense of safety, or the quiet sting of realizing you weren't fully there when it mattered.

Time doesn't preserve what happened.

It preserves how it landed.

Regret rarely comes from mistakes the way people assume. It doesn't usually come from trying and failing.

You can recover from professional failures.

You can rebuild careers. You can re-earn money.

Those losses are tangible, and tangible things can be replaced.

Regret comes from emotional negligence. From the apology you delayed because pride felt easier. From the warmth you withheld because distance felt safer. From choosing to win instead of understand. From silence you justified as strength.

Emotional moments are one-time events. Once missed, they don't return in the same form.

The opportunity might come back. The moment doesn't.

And what lingers later isn't what the other person did or didn't do.

It's who you were in that moment.
This isn't about being perfect.

Making every moment "good" doesn't mean being kind all the time, suppressing anger, or tolerating disrespect.

It means being conscious. Aware enough to recognize that what you're about to say or do will likely become a memory yours or someone else's.

Not in terms of pride, but in terms of peace.

Care is often reserved for people who feel familiar or safe.

But memories don't work that way. A harsh word to a stranger can sit heavier than silence from a friend.

An unnecessary cruelty toward someone you dislike can linger longer than their wrongdoing. Because regret isn't really about them. It's about knowing you acted in a way that didn't align with who you want to be when no one was keeping a score.

Emotional actions age faster than time.

Professional decisions age with relevance.

Emotional decisions age with conscience.

What felt justified at twenty-two can feel unnecessary at thirty-two. What felt powerful in the moment can feel hollow later. That's why emotional maturity isn't about control.

It's about foresight seeing the future version of yourself sitting alone with a memory and acting in a way that won't make that person flinch.

Most wisdom is simple. That's why it's avoided. Before reacting, before speaking, before withdrawing, there is often a small opening.

A pause. A breath.

Not to calculate advantage or look composed, but to remember that this moment is quietly becoming a memory.

You don't need to make it dramatic.
You just need to make it clean.

Life isn't measured by milestones. It's measured by how safe your memories feel when you sit alone with them.

So don't aim to be flawless. Aim to be intentional.

Let your future self-look back and say honestly that you may not have done everything right,

but you showed up with warmth, courage, and care.

That is what remains.
Everything else fades.

What you delay today becomes regret later.

-Be More Human-

People Are Trying

We live in a world where people comment on lives they do not carry. Everyone has an opinion. Everyone has a verdict ready. Very few have the patience to understand what it actually takes to be someone to wake up inside a mind,

To carry a history, to move through days shaped by things that were never chosen.

Judgment has become casual. It moves quickly. It travels far. It rarely asks for context. From a distance, it is easy to name what looks broken. A weakness here. An insecurity there. A flaw disguised as "honesty." The words sound sharp. Confident. Sometimes even principled.

But most of the time, it is not honesty.

It is distance.

It is the safety of not being responsible for the impact of what is said. When you do not carry the weight of another person's reality, it is easy to speak freely. When you do not live with the consequences, precision feels optional. Care feels unnecessary.

Criticism offered without responsibility is not truth-telling. It is detachment.

When you speak without any willingness to stay, to help, or to carry what your words create, you are not revealing truth. You are releasing an observation and stepping away from its impact. That distance is the difference. Truth accepts responsibility for where it lands. Detachment does not.

If you cannot support someone, you have no real place in criticising them. Not because people should be shielded from truth, but because truth is not neutral. It enters a person already carrying context you do not fully see. Without care, words do not clarify. They apply pressure. They expose without providing ground.

Truth without care does not guide.
It overwhelms.

This is why it becomes violent not in intent, but in effect. It disrupts without offering stability. It names without helping integrate. The language may be accurate. It may even be correct. But correctness alone is not humane.

That is what makes it violence with better grammar.

Not cruelty, but refusal. The refusal to be responsible for what follows. The ease of saying something sharp while remaining untouched by its consequences. Words like this do not open people. They close them.

Truth that cannot stay is not truth meant to help.
It is truth used to exit.

There is a difference between seeing someone and helping them. And simply looking at them long enough to judge.

Anyone can notice a crack.

Anyone can point to what seems misaligned.

That takes no intimacy. No risk. No patience.

It takes a different kind of human to understand what it feels like to live inside the crack.

People do not carry their fears openly. They learn early that fear is inconvenient, unattractive, difficult to explain.

So, it gets buried. It hides in jokes that go a little too far. In silence that lasts longer than it should. In overwork. In anger. In distraction. In confidence that feels rehearsed.

What is often labelled as weakness is usually someone surviving something that never made it into language. What is called insecurity is often a wound that never found safety. These things do not announce themselves clearly. They distort behaviour instead.

And behaviour is what gets judged.

Words spoken from a distance flatten complexity. They reduce entire lives into moments. Reactions into character. Struggle into failure. This reduction feels efficient. It feels intelligent. But it is rarely accurate.

When you speak without the intention to lift, you are not being brave.

You are being careless.

And careless words do not make you sharp. They make you small. They cost nothing to deliver and offer nothing in return. They leave weight behind without carrying any of it themselves.

There is a quiet dignity in choosing to be kind.

Not performative kindness. Not visible generosity. Not the kind that seeks acknowledgment. But restraint. The simple act of not adding weight to someone who is already carrying enough. The decision to pause instead of press. To soften instead of sharpen.

Kindness like this rarely gets noticed.

But it gets felt.

You do not have to understand everything someone is dealing with. Understanding fully is often impossible. But you do have to decide what kind of presence you want to be in another person's life.

Presence is not neutral.
It either adds pressure or creates space.
If you speak, speak with something that builds.
If you cannot build, at least do not destroy.

Sometimes the most human thing you can offer is not advice.
Not critique.
Not opinion.
But space.

Space for someone to be unfinished. Space for someone to change without being punished for who they were yesterday. Space to exist without having to defend themselves constantly.

This kind of space is rare.

It asks for patience in a culture that rewards immediacy. It asks for restraint in a world that mistakes reaction for honesty. It asks for maturity in situations where dominance would be easier.

Kindness is not weakness.
Silence is not avoidance.
Restraint is not passivity.
They are forms of respect.

They signal that you recognise the limits of your perspective. That you understand how partial your view is. That you are aware that someone else's inner world is larger than the fragment you are allowed to see.

Every person is already fighting something you cannot see. Every mind carries stories you will never fully understand or relate to.

When you choose to speak with care, you are not simply being polite.

You are becoming a place of safety.

That safety does not fix anyone.

It does not solve their problems.

But it allows them to breathe. It allows them to remain intact while they figure things out. It gives them room to keep trying without fear of being torn down for not having arrived yet.

And trying is not nothing.

Sometimes the greatest support is simply allowing someone to exist without judgment for who they are becoming. Without freezing them in their worst moment. Without turning their struggle into a spectacle.

If you cannot support someone, let them be.

Give them the dignity of their own process.

Their own pace.

Their own learning curve.

Life already applies enough pressure. It does not need additional weight from people who are not invested in the outcome. And if you choose to speak, let it be in a way that reminds them they are not alone.

Not broken.

Not unworthy of patience.

Words can either close a person in or open them back to themselves.

Choose the kind that opens.

Most people are just doing the best they know how.

-Be More Human-

Be The Admirer

Indifference often passes as maturity. Being unbothered is treated like control. Detachment is mistaken for strength. People move through life as if nothing should reach them, as if being affected by something is a liability rather than a sign of awareness.

At some point, admiration began to feel unnecessary.

Beauty appears and is dismissed without pause. Depth is skimmed without letting it settle. Effort is met with irony and renamed peace.

But peace does not come from ignoring life. It comes from the ability to stay with it.

From noticing without immediately needing to explain, rank, or reduce what appears. Indifference feels safe. If nothing moves you, nothing can disappoint you.

If nothing impresses you, nothing can unsettle your sense of self.

This distance looks composed from the outside, but inside it often feels flat.

Quiet without richness.

Calm without depth.

Life does not become dull on its own. Attention withdraws.

Admiration requires pause. It asks for presence.

It asks you to acknowledge that something outside you has weight. A sunset that slows you unexpectedly. A piece of work shaped by patience. A moment that carries sincerity without demanding reaction. These moments do not ask for performance.

They ask to be recognised.

Recognition, however, feels vulnerable. To admire is to admit that something touched you. And vulnerability, when control is mistaken for wisdom, feels risky. So, admiration is replaced with distance.

With sarcasm.

With judgment.

With the posture of not caring too much.

This withdrawal does not stop with life itself. It extends to people.

Discipline goes unnoticed. Quiet endurance is overlooked. Consistency without spectacle disappears into the background. Small acts of kindness pass without acknowledgment. Instead of appreciation, there is critique. Instead of curiosity, there is comparison. Instead of recognition, reduction.

Judgment is easier than admiration.

Judgment keeps you above. Admiration places you alongside. Standing alongside someone means accepting that they carry something you may not. That they reached a place through effort, clarity, or persistence. That acknowledgment can feel threatening when worth is tied to remaining untouched.

But admiring someone does not make you lesser.

It means you still recognise value when it appears.

Admiration does not demand imitation.

It does not require agreement. It does not diminish you.

It simply acknowledges reality.

Someone showed up. Someone stayed. Someone tried where disengagement would have been easier.

To notice that is not softness.

It is awareness.

When admiration fades, perception dulls.

Everything begins to feel interchangeable. People blur together. Moments lose texture. You may feel protected, but you also feel less alive.

The world becomes quieter, but also thinner.

Being unmoved is not the same as being stable.

Stability can hold feeling without being overwhelmed by it. Indifference avoids feeling altogether.

One is grounded. The other is withdrawn.

One keeps you present. The other slowly removes you from participation.

Admiration does not destabilise.

It grounds.

It keeps perception awake. It reminds you that you are still in contact with what is real. That attention has not fully retreated inward. That something outside you can still slow you down without threatening you.

This is why admiration feels energising rather than draining. It reconnects you to meaning without demanding explanation. It sharpens without hardening. It deepens without overwhelming. It is quiet, but it is alive.

The habit of pretending nothing impresses you erodes this aliveness slowly. Pauses disappear. Lingering feels unnecessary. Things matter only when they serve you directly. Life continues, but it does not land.

Peace is not the absence of feeling.

It is the ability to feel without losing yourself.

Admiration practices this ability. It allows you to be moved without being shaken.

To see beauty without needing to own it.

To recognise strength without competing with it.

To notice effort without diminishing your own.

This does not make life dramatic. It makes it textured. It restores contrast. It allows meaning to return without being forced.

Those who truly live are not untouched by the world. They are not protected by distance. They are not defined by how little affects them.

They remain receptive. They allow themselves to be impressed without embarrassment.

They pause when something deserves it. They acknowledge effort when they see it.
They let moments register instead of passing through untouched. That does not make them naïve.

It makes them present. Presence is not loud. It does not announce itself.

It is revealed in attention. In the willingness to notice. In the refusal to flatten everything into indifference.

Let life register again.

Let people register again.

Not everything needs to be filtered out.

Some things deserve to be admired.

Caring keeps life from going dull.

-Be More Human-

Choosing The Good Even When It's Bad

People are rarely good or bad. They are unfinished. Still forming. Still reacting to things that shaped them unevenly. Yet attention is often spent scanning for flaws—who lied, who disappointed, who failed to show up the way they were expected to. This scanning feels responsible. It feels like awareness. Like self-protection.

Over time, it becomes something heavier.

The habit of searching for what is wrong trains the mind to live in suspicion. Suspicion narrows perception. It keeps the inner world braced. Even before anything happens, disappointment is already anticipated. The body remains tense, the mind alert, always preparing for the next confirmation that distance was justified.

Suspicion is heavy to carry.

Looking for the good in people—even in those who have caused harm is often misunderstood. It is assumed to mean excusing behaviour, overlooking damage, or surrendering boundaries. But that is not what it is. It is not denial. It is not naïveté. It is not permission for harm to repeat.

It is a decision about the kind of inner world you are willing to live inside.

Judgment poisons the observer before it ever reaches the observed. Not dramatically. Gradually. Each time someone is reduced to their worst moment, perspective shrinks. The mind becomes trapped in reaction. Other people's darkness begins to determine your internal weather.

Over time, this creates a posture. Cynical. Closed. Always waiting. Even neutral moments feel charged, because disappointment is already expected. Nothing has happened yet, but the mind is prepared for impact.

This is how bitterness settles in. Not through a single betrayal, but through repeated identification with judgment.

Choosing to look for the good interrupts this pattern.

When attention shifts, something subtle changes. Conclusions loosen. Context comes into view. Pain appears before intent. Fear appears before malice. Confusion appears before strategy. This does not make harmful behaviour acceptable.

It makes it understandable.

Understanding is not approval.

It is release.

When you understand without absorbing, you loosen the grip that other people's actions have on your inner state. You stop carrying resentment that does not protect you. You stop reliving harm in the name of vigilance. You acknowledge what happened without letting it dictate how you see everything that follows.

This does not mean trusting everyone.

It means understanding without absorbing.

Boundaries remain. Distance remains when it is necessary. But the heart does not harden in the process. There is a quiet strength in saying: I see your flaws, and I refuse to let them turn me bitter.

That refusal is not passive.

It is authority over your inner world.

A steady inner state is not built by pretending everything is good. It is built by choosing where attention rests. Again, and again. Even when judgment feels easier. Even when empathy feels uncomfortable. Even when suspicion seems justified.

Judgment offers quick certainty. Empathy does not. Empathy asks you to stay with complexity. To hold contradiction. To see clearly without simplifying a person into a label.

That takes discipline.

But discipline directed inward changes the quality of life outward.

The world has not suddenly become harsher.

Judgment has simply become faster.

Conclusions are drawn before context arrives. Labels replace understanding. Outrage replaces clarity. The inner world mirrors that speed, becoming reactive instead of spacious.

Each time empathy is chosen over contempt, something returns. Each time clarity replaces outrage, the mind lightens. Each time understanding replaces labelling, a measure of peace is reclaimed.

Not for them.

For you.

Because the goal is not to fix people. That task is endless. The goal is to remain human while moving through a world that constantly pressures you to shrink into certainty, into defensiveness, into distance.

Remaining human does not mean remaining unguarded. It means staying open without being unprotected. It means allowing nuance without surrendering self-respect. It means seeing people as incomplete rather than irredeemable.

This does not make life easier in the short term.

It makes it steadier over time.

When the mind stops scanning for disappointment, attention frees up. You begin to notice what is working. What is sincere. What is trying. Not because everything deserves praise, but because constant vigilance drains more than it protects.

Carrying bitterness does not make you safer. It makes you smaller. It narrows perception. It keeps the nervous system on edge. Choosing the good even when it is hard is not moral superiority.

It is self-preservation.

You are allowed to acknowledge harm without becoming hardened by it. You are allowed to protect yourself without poisoning your own perception. You are allowed to understand without excusing, to empathise without surrendering boundaries.

This balance is quiet. It does not announce itself. But it changes how you move through people, conflict, and uncertainty. You respond instead of react. You see before you decide. You remain intact even when others are not.

That integrity matters.

Because the inner world you cultivate becomes the lens through which everything else is experienced. And a lens shaped by suspicion will always distort, no matter how justified it feels.

Choosing the good is not optimism.

It is discipline.

A discipline of attention. A discipline of perspective.
A discipline of refusing to let another person's worst moment
decide your inner state.

Each time you choose it, you choose yourself.

Not the hardened version. Not the defended one. But the one that can still see clearly, still feel deeply, and still remain open without losing ground.

That is not softness. That is strength.

Holding bitterness costs more than letting it go.

-Be More Human-

Outgrowing AS BETRAYAL

Not everything that ends is broken.

Some connections don't collapse. They don't fracture under conflict or dissolve through harm. They loosen instead. Quietly. Without a moment you can point to and say, *this is where it changed.* One day you simply notice that the conversation doesn't go where it used to. The rhythm feels unfamiliar. The effort feels heavier than the meaning.

Nothing dramatic happened.

And yet, something is no longer aligned.

This shift is often mistaken for disloyalty.

Staying is treated as proof of care. Distance is expected to come with an explanation. Continuity is seen as virtue. If something mattered once, it is assumed it must continue to matter in the same way. When it doesn't, the change feels suspicious, even when no one has done anything wrong.

But growth does not always move in groups.

When it doesn't, separation begins to resemble betrayal not because harm occurred, but because the change has no clear reason. There is no argument to point to. No moment that explains the distance. Just a quiet awareness that something has shifted.

Outgrowing rarely arrives with clarity. It comes first as discomfort. As hesitation. You notice yourself editing what you say, not out of fear, but because the words no longer land the same way.

What once felt shared now feels translated.

You are still understood, but not instinctively.

The connection hasn't disappeared.

It has changed shape.

There is grief in this, but it is not loud. It doesn't announce itself. You don't miss the person as much as you miss the ease. The unspoken understanding. The version of yourself that existed naturally around them.

That loss is subtle, which makes it harder to accept.

So, continuity is often forced.

You keep showing up the same way even when something inside has moved. You keep the rhythm alive even when it no longer fits. Presence slowly turns into effort. Conversation turns into maintenance. Nothing ends, but something begins to wear thin.

This quiet strain is confusing, because there is no one to blame.

Outgrowing is not about superiority. It is not about depth or pace or becoming "better." It is simply the recognition that people move differently. That alignment changes. That what once felt natural can start feeling slightly off without becoming wrong.

What makes this difficult is the absence of blame.

There is no clean narrative. No justification that makes the distance feel acceptable. Just the recognition that the space between you has changed shape. And because it changed without permission, it feels wrong even when it is honest.

Some connections belong to a season. They make sense while you are becoming. Holding onto them beyond that season doesn't preserve them. It distorts them. You begin asking the past to behave like the present.

You ask people to meet you where they never agreed to go.

Letting go without resentment is not weakness.

It is accuracy.

The relationship doesn't disappear. It doesn't need to be erased or rewritten. It simply becomes different. Less immediate. Less central. Still real, just no longer asking for the same closeness. And recognizing that without turning it into a story of fault is not betrayal.

It is awareness.

Some things end without being wrong.

-Be More Human

Leaving Is Not Failure

Leaving is not something you do because you stopped caring. It is not a signal that something was shallow, replaceable, or meaningless. You leave because time moved, and you moved with it. That is the part we struggle to accept. We want meaning to guarantee permanence. We want depth to promise longevity. But life does not make those agreements. It never has.

Most of us fight this truth quietly. We don't deny it openly; we resist it internally. We pretend permanence is possible if we hold tighter, remember harder, explain ourselves better. We tell ourselves that if something mattered enough, it should have stayed intact. If it didn't, then someone must have failed. Someone must have quit. Someone must have been careless. This belief is comforting because it gives loss a villain. But life does not operate on blame. People change rooms. Places outgrow us. Seasons close without asking permission.

Leaving is not the betrayal we make it out to be. More often than not, it is simply the natural conclusion of attention shifting. What once required your full presence slowly stops asking for it. Not dramatically. Not cruelly. Just quietly, until one day you realize you are staying out of habit rather than alignment. That moment is rarely loud, but it is honest.

What hurts is not the departure itself. What hurts is the mind refusing to let the moment end.

The body adapts faster than the mind. You physically leave places long before you mentally exit them. This is where the real friction begins. We replay conversations that are already finished, as though repeating them might produce a different outcome. We mentally sit in places we no longer belong, imagining ourselves there as if nothing has changed. We ask "what if" questions to people who are no longer listening. We keep negotiating with versions of reality that have already moved on.

This is where suffering takes root. Not in loss, but in fixation.

There is an important difference between carrying memory and living inside it, though the two often feel similar at first. Memory is allowed to be emotional. It is allowed to soften you. It is allowed to visit unexpectedly, like a familiar song, a smell that pauses your breath, or a sentence that suddenly reminds you of who you were. That kind of remembering is human. It does not ask you to go backwards. It simply acknowledges that something left a mark.

Fixation is different. Fixation freezes life at a point that has already passed. It demands that the present behave like the past. It insists that today must feel the way yesterday did, even though the conditions that created yesterday no longer exist. Fixation turns memory into a standard rather than a reference, and the present inevitably fails that comparison.

The present always loses when it is forced to compete with a memory. Not because it is inferior, but because it is alive, unfinished, and unresolved. Memory is polished by distance. The present is still rough.

Some people were meant to meet you, not stay. Some places were meant to shape you, not house you forever. Their role was real, even if temporary. This is one of the most difficult truths to accept because it disrupts the story, we like to tell ourselves about meaning. We assume that significance must equal permanence. That if something mattered deeply, it should remain indefinitely. But life does not measure importance that way.

Not everything meaningful is permanent.

Not everything permanent is meaningful.

We rarely question the first statement. We struggle with the second.

When you accept this, something loosens inside you. Not all at once, and not dramatically, but subtly. You stop gripping old versions of yourself that no longer fit. You stop punishing new moments for not feeling like old ones. You stop measuring today by yesterday's emotions, which were shaped by circumstances that no longer exist.

Leaving does not erase what was felt. Distance does not invalidate connection. Endings do not cancel depth. They complete it. Completion is not the same as failure, even though we often confuse the two. Failure implies something was cut short or mishandled. Completion simply means something reached its natural conclusion.

We struggle with this distinction because we equate endurance with success. Staying feels noble. Leaving feels suspicious. But endurance without alignment becomes self-betrayal, and staying long after something has ended internally only creates resentment where there was once care.

You do not need to mentally revisit every goodbye to honor it. You do not need to suffer to prove something mattered. Pain is not proof of depth. What mattered already happened. It lived, it shaped you, and it left its trace. Demanding that it stay alive in your mind forever does not make it more real. It only makes you less present.

Memory was never meant to be a residence. It was meant to be a place you can visit.

There is a quiet cruelty in forcing yourself to remain emotionally loyal to moments that have already released you. You think you are being respectful. You think you are being faithful. But often, you are simply afraid of allowing space for something new to exist without comparison. You are afraid that moving forward might look like betrayal, when in reality it is acknowledgment.

Carrying warmth does not require carrying weight. You can remember without reliving. You can honor without returning. You can be shaped by something without being defined by it forever. This is not detachment. It is maturity.

Maturity is not emotional numbness. It is emotional accuracy. It is knowing when to feel fully and when to let go cleanly. It is recognizing that clinging does not preserve meaning; it distorts it. When you hold something beyond its time, you don't keep it alive. You change its shape.

To be human is not to cling endlessly. It is to feel deeply and still walk forward. It is to allow experiences to end without rewriting them as failures. It is to trust that life is not subtracting from you when something leaves, but rearranging what needs to come next.

Sometimes, walking forward is the most respectful thing you can do for what once was. Not because it didn't matter, but because it mattered enough to be complete.

The Distance That Comes After Clarity

There is a kind of distance that comes from being pushed away. And then there is another kind the one that appears when you begin to see clearly.

It doesn't announce itself.
It doesn't feel dramatic or heavy.

Life continues. Conversations happen. People remain around you. And yet something subtle has rearranged itself beneath the surface. You are present, but not entangled in the same way anymore.

This distance doesn't come from rejection.
It comes from alignment.

When you stop exaggerating reactions, when you no longer rush to agree, when you step out of performance disguised as participation, space forms naturally. Not because others withdrew, but because you stopped leaning forward unnecessarily.

What appears isn't cold or hostile.

It's clean.

Clarity does this. It removes urgency. It removes the pressure to constantly signal who you are. And without those signals, many connections loosen on their own.

You notice it in small ways.

You listen more than you speak.
You respond without immediacy.
Silence no longer feels like something to escape.

Some conversations end sooner. Some invitations arrive less frequently. Not out of intent simply because your rhythm no longer matches what it once did.

This is where confusion often enters.

The mind searches for explanations. It wants to frame the distance as withdrawal, emotional detachment, or quiet arrogance. But those labels miss the truth.

What's happening is simpler.

You are no longer forcing compatibility.

Clarity doesn't separate you from people.
It separates you from pretence.

And that separation can feel unfamiliar in a world built on constant engagement. When participation slows, when noise recedes, you find yourself with more space than before.

Not as punishment.
As consequence.

This part is rarely acknowledged. Awareness is often described as freedom, but it also brings restraint. You become careful with words. Selective with reactions. Intentional with attachments.

You stop borrowing emotions just to stay included. You stop mistaking stimulation for connection.

And quietly, without ceremony, you step out of shared illusions.

The distance that follows isn't emptiness.

It's margin.

Margin where reflex once lived.
Margin where noise used to settle.
Margin that feels unfamiliar only because it isn't filled automatically anymore.

If you rush to close this space, you'll misread it. You'll try to fill it with distraction, explanation, or old patterns. But if you remain steady, something shifts.

The distance stops feeling sharp.

It becomes neutral.
Grounded.
Clear.

You realize you are not cut off from life.
You are simply no longer crowded by it.

Clarity doesn't make life smaller.
It removes what never belonged.

The distance you feel is not a sign that something is wrong. It is the space left behind when you stop performing closeness that wasn't true. When you no longer rush to be understood. When you allow connections to exist without forcing them to stay the same.

What remains is quieter.
But it is also real.

You are not stepping away from people.
You are stepping back into proportion.

And in that proportion, something steadies. You stop mistaking noise for connection, presence for effort, or closeness for honesty. You let space exist without trying to fill it.

Not everything needs to follow you forward. Some things are meant to loosen, so you can walk without dragging parts of yourself that no longer move with you.

That distance is not absence.

It is alignment, finally allowed to breathe.

Clarity creates space for you to think, not coldness.

-Be More Human-

Not Caring Feels Better

There comes a point where things stop reaching you the way they once did. Not because you have understood them fully, and not because they have lost their importance, but because you have learned to step back before they ask anything of you. You sense the moment earlier now. Before the pull. Before the reaction. Before the quiet demand to feel, respond, or explain. Reactions soften.

Opinions lose their edge.

The impulse to engage grows quieter. What looks from the outside like neutrality or balance is often just distance that has settled in and learned how to remain.

This state rarely arrives with drama. It forms slowly, after caring begins to feel repetitive or unrewarded. When effort is offered again and again without response, when attention does not change outcomes, something in the mind adjusts. Not consciously.

It adapts. It learns to conserve. It learns that less response costs less. Less involvement feels efficient. Less exposure feels controlled. Over time, this distance begins to resemble strength, even though it is closer to withdrawal than clarity.

This is why it can be mistaken for peace.

Before calling it calm, it helps to look again. Sometimes what arrives is not calm at all, but the absence of feeling, and that absence is welcomed because it hurts less. Caring keeps you open. It leaves you available to disappointment, misunderstanding, and loss. Not caring closes that door quietly. Nothing presses as hard anymore. Nothing reaches deep enough to disturb you. And in that relief, numbness feels earned, even responsible.

Apathy often passes as calm because the surface looks similar. Both are quiet. Both avoid excess. Both reduce friction. But calm still pays attention. It stays present. It notices what is happening and chooses how to respond.

Apathy does not choose. It avoids decision by avoiding attachment. It removes itself from the equation entirely, not as an act of wisdom, but as a way to stop being asked anything at all.

At first, this feels lighter. Expectations drop. Disappointment loses its sharpness. The emotional load becomes easier to carry because it is smaller. Life becomes more manageable when nothing matters enough to disturb it deeply. But something else fades alongside that manageability. Curiosity dulls. Presence thins. Engagement weakens. Life continues, but at a distance, as if observed rather than lived.

The world does not disappear.

It just feels farther away.

This distance is subtle, which is why it often goes unnoticed. There is no clear moment where you can say, this is when I stopped caring. There is only a gradual quieting. A steady reduction in response. You still show up. You still function. But something essential has stepped back, and because the pain has reduced, the loss is easy to overlook.

Humans are not meant to exist untouched by what surrounds them.

We are shaped through response, not absence.

Even restraint requires engagement.

Even detachment, when it is healthy, is conscious and temporary.

It is chosen, held, and released.

Apathy is different. It lingers because it is rarely questioned. It settles in without resistance and begins to define the tone of days without ever announcing itself.

This does not mean everything deserves a reaction. It does not mean staying emotionally exposed or carrying every weight that passes by. It does not mean intensity is required for meaning. It simply means disappearing from your own experience is not the same as mastering it. When nothing reaches you anymore, it may feel like control, but it often signals that something vital has gone quiet.

There is a difference between choosing distance and defaulting to it.

When distance is chosen, it remains flexible. It can open and close. It responds to context. When distance becomes habitual, it hardens.

It stops adjusting.

It becomes the baseline.

You don't pull back because it is appropriate.

You pull back because it is familiar.

The opposite of apathy is not intensity.

It is participation. Participation does not need to be loud. It does not need to be constant.

It simply means remaining present enough to be affected. To let something land. To let something matter, even briefly.

Participation is where meaning quietly survives.

Not in constant engagement, but in selective presence.

In moments where you allow yourself to respond instead of withdraw. In choosing not to disappear just because distance feels easier.

Meaning does not require emotional excess.

It requires contact.

Not caring can feel better for a while.

It smooths the surface.

It reduces friction.

It makes life easier to manage.

But over time, it also reduces depth.

And without depth, life does not become peaceful.

It becomes distant.

Feeling less is easier, but it isn't peace.

-Be More Human-

ACT IV
(Quiet Disciplines)

Listen What You Speak

What you say matters more than it appears to. Not in a mystical sense, and not as motivation, but as consequence. Words are not harmless because they are familiar. The ones you repeat quietly, casually, without attention, train the mind in how to interpret what it meets. Over time, they become the tone through which reality is filtered.

Speak in complaint, and life slowly begins to feel adversarial. Speak in bitterness, and events start to feel personal. Speak lightly, negatively, without care, and the inner world begins to mirror that carelessness.

Not dramatically. Gradually.

Most people assume thoughts shape words. In practice, it moves both ways. What you speak returns to you as belief. Language does not merely describe experience; it reinforces it. Repeated long enough, it becomes familiar.

Familiar enough, it becomes accepted. And what is accepted eventually feels true.

This is why two people can live the same life and experience it differently. The difference is rarely circumstance. It is reinforcement. One keeps naming decay. The other keeps naming steadiness. Over time, both feel confirmed.

Language settles into identity quietly. You don't wake up one day changed.

You wake up inside a world that sounds the way you've been speaking about it.

Ancient Hindu thought understood this long before psychology tried to quantify it.

There is a story less a myth than a reminder about where power truly resides. The gods once considered where to place the most potent force in existence. A force capable of creation or destruction, depending on how it was used. Something subtle enough to go unnoticed, yet strong enough to shape destiny.

Some proposed hiding it in the depths of the ocean, beyond human reach. Others believed it should be placed atop the highest mountains, where only the most disciplined could approach it. But both ideas were dismissed. Any power hidden outside the human would eventually be found.

Humans have always conquered distance.

So, a different choice was made.

The power was placed within the human itself.

On the tongue.

Because the tongue moves before the mind fully settles. It reveals intention before action. It exposes alignment without effort.

The gods understood something simple: humans would guard gold, weapons, and knowledge,

but rarely their own speech.

And so, the most consequential force was entrusted to the place humans used most casually.

This was not a punishment.

It was trust.

What you repeatedly speak becomes what you slowly accept.
What you accept becomes what you tolerate.

And what you tolerate shapes the life you live.

Not all at once. Not visibly. But steadily, until the environment you inhabit internally begins to resemble the language you live in.

This is not about forced positivity. It is not about pretending everything is good, or masking difficulty with optimism. Speaking well does not mean lying to yourself.

It means not poisoning yourself unnecessarily.

It means not weakening your own footing through careless repetition.

There is a difference between acknowledging difficulty and rehearsing defeat.

Between naming pain and building an identity around it. Between honesty and indulgence. The tongue does not know the difference **unless attention is present.**

Life listens less to what you want and more to what you keep affirming. Not because life is sentient in a mystical sense,

but because the mind aligns itself with what it hears repeatedly.

And most people affirm their limitations daily.

Casually. Without noticing.

Speech is where inner posture becomes external habit.

You hear it in the way people talk about time, about effort, about themselves.

Everything is exhausting.

Everything is unfair.

Everything is pointless.

Over time, this language does not remain commentary.

It becomes climate.

And the climate shapes how energy moves, how decisions are made, how long effort is sustained before it is abandoned.

None of this is dramatic.
That is why it works.

The most influential forces are rarely loud. They are consistent. They are close. They are always present. Speech is one of them. It is the interface between inner life and outer reality. It bridges thought and action without friction.

And because it feels harmless, it goes unguarded.

The power was never hidden from you.
It was trusted to you.

Not because humans are careful, but because they are careless. And carelessness with something powerful has consequences that look ordinary while they are forming.

By the time they are noticed, they feel like fate.

The way you speak is the way you shape what stays with

YOU.
Not instantly.
Not magically.
But inevitably.

Nothing more. Nothing less.

The way you talk becomes the way you live.

-Be More Human-

Don't Name Every Struggle

There is a habit that has grown quietly over time. Almost unnoticed. Everything that passes through the inner world is named. Stress becomes a label. Sadness becomes a condition. Confusion becomes an identity. At first, this feels relieving. Naming discomfort gives the sense that something has been contained. If it has a name, it feels manageable. Explainable. Almost solved.

But somewhere along the way, naming stopped being a way to notice and became a way to cling.

The experience itself did not deepen.
The relationship to it changed.

When every emotional shift is immediately translated into language, something subtle happens. Attention narrows. The mind circles inward. Instead of passing through an experience, it begins to watch it. Track it. Revisit it. What was once a passing state starts to feel fixed. Not because the feeling is stronger, but because it has been given shape before it had time to move.

Not every low phase needs a diagnosis.
Not every heavy day needs interpretation.

Sometimes the mind is not asking to be understood. It is asking to be left alone long enough to settle.

There is a difference between noticing an emotion and narrating it. Noticing allows movement. Narration often interrupts it. When an inner state is repeatedly named, discussed, and framed as *something I have*, it stays active longer.

Language gives it edges.

Definition gives it weight. What could have softened on its own is kept alive through repetition.

The feeling lingers not because it is powerful, but because it is being observed too closely.

This is not because emotions are imagined or exaggerated. They are real.

But they are also temporary by nature.

They rise, signal, and dissolve. That is their design. What interferes with this process is constant commentary. The mind does not let the emotion complete its cycle. It holds it open.

There is a reason emotional states move differently in children. Not because children feel less, but because they do not rehearse what they feel.

They experience fully, and then attention shifts. There is no inner monologue asking what this says about them. No vocabulary being assembled around the discomfort. The emotion arrives, peaks, and leaves.

Adulthood reverses this pattern.

The feeling arrives, and instead of passing, it is explained. Then explained again. Then contextualised.

Then shared.

Then mirrored back through content, conversation, and memory. The emotion is no longer just felt. It is maintained. Protected. Reinforced.

What began as a moment becomes a story. What was once movement becomes position.

This is how temporary states harden into identities. Not through intensity, but through repetition. The mind grows attached to what it keeps naming. Familiarity settles in. And familiarity is persuasive. The emotion begins to feel like something that belongs.

Healing does not always come from understanding more. Sometimes it comes from saying less. From letting the nervous system recalibrate without being translated into thought every few minutes.

Silence allows something analysis cannot.

It allows emotions to finish what they started.

This silence is often misunderstood.

It is not avoidance.
It is not denial.
It is not repression.

Suppression is pretending something is not there. Silence is allowing it to be there without building a structure around it. Silence is restraint. It is the recognition that not every experience benefits from language. Some experiences resolve only when they are not given a microphone.

There is also a quiet strength in not turning every inner struggle into a public explanation.

When you resist the urge to define yourself immediately, you leave room to change.

You do not corner your future self into staying the same. You do not freeze a moment into meaning.

Language has a way of making things feel permanent.

Once something is named often enough, it begins to sound stable.

Predictable.

As if it has always been there. The mind starts expecting it. Preparing for it.

What you expect, you notice faster.
What you notice faster, you reinforce.
This is not because the mind is weak.
It is because it learns through attention.

Reflection has its place. But reflection that never ends becomes rumination. And rumination does not heal. It keeps the system unfinished.

Alert.
Waiting.

The mind stays busy, but the body never settles.

Some days, the healthiest response is not

what is this?
*It is this will pa*ss.

And then attention returns elsewhere. Not as avoidance, but as grounding. To the body. To routine. To movement. To ordinary life. Not everything needs to be processed at the level of meaning. Some things need to be lived through until they lose their charge.

Ordinary actions do this quietly. Walking. Working. Eating. Sleeping. Repetition restores proportion. It reminds the system that not every internal shift requires interpretation. Some sensations dissolve simply because time and neutrality were allowed to do their work.

This is why silence has always been part of healing, even before it had language around it.

Silence reduces friction.

It stops the constant reactivation of the same emotional loop.
It lets the system reset without interference.

Modern life rarely allows this. Everything is shared, named, archived. Every feeling is turned into content. Every moment is given context before it has ended.

The inner world becomes crowded with commentary.

And crowded systems struggle to regulate.

Not everything needs to be named.
Not every feeling needs to be quoted.

Some experiences dissolve only when they are not held up to the light. When they are allowed to be incomplete. Unfinished. Unexplained. When the mind steps back and lets the body carry what it knows how to carry.

This does not make emotions smaller.
It makes them mobile.

They move when they are not confined.

There is intelligence in knowing when to reflect and when to remain silent. When to examine and when to trust that the system knows how to return to balance on its own. This intelligence is not dramatic. It does not announce itself. It looks like restraint. Like patience. Like letting something pass without demanding that it justify itself.

Some things heal because they were understood.

Some things heal because they were not disturbed.

And knowing the difference is not weakness.
It is discernment.

Some feelings pass faster when you don't hold them.

-Be More Human-

The Discipline Of Questioning Yourself

Beliefs are rarely held lightly. Once formed, they are defended like property. Guarded. Inherited. Rarely inspected. A conviction, once settled, becomes a place of comfort not because it is necessarily true, but because it is familiar. Familiarity creates safety. Safety creates attachment. And attachment quietly replaces inquiry.

At some point, questioning stops. Not because answers were found, but because certainty feels easier than doubt. We stop asking how a belief was built and begin assuming it must be right simply because it has been carried for a long time. Time lends legitimacy. Repetition lends authority. And soon, the belief is no longer an idea it is part of identity.

This is where growth usually slows.

Growth does not begin with confidence. It begins with discomfort. Specifically, the discomfort of turning attention inward and asking whether what you believe still deserves to be believed. Putting your own convictions on trial feels destabilizing because it removes the ground you have been standing on. But without that moment of instability, nothing actually changes.

Challenging your beliefs does not mean abandoning them. It means testing their strength. A belief that collapses under questioning was never a foundation. It was a habit. Something repeated often enough to feel solid, but never examined closely enough to be reliable.

Friction is how structure is revealed.

When ideas are exposed to contradiction, disagreement, or unfamiliar perspectives, their weaknesses show themselves.

Sometimes they bend and adapt. Sometimes they sharpen. And sometimes they break entirely. None of these outcomes are failures. What fails is refusing to look.

Opposing views are often treated as threats.

As something to defend against, dismiss, or defeat. But opposition is not inherently hostile. It is informative. It highlights angles your agreement could never show you. Where everyone agrees, nothing is questioned.

Where nothing is questioned, nothing evolves.

Disagreement is not an attack on your intelligence.

It is an invitation to expand it.

Listening to someone who sees the world differently requires restraint. The impulse to interrupt, correct, or retreat appears quickly. Dismissing them is easy. Listening without preparing a rebuttal is not. That requires patience. It requires the ability to hold uncertainty without rushing to close it.

This is why questioning yourself is a discipline, not a trait.

It does not come naturally. The ego resists it. The ego prefers consistency over accuracy, certainty over truth. Being right feels stable. Being uncertain feels exposed. And so, rigidity often masquerades as conviction.

True conviction is not rigid.

It is flexible. It adapts when presented with better evidence. It refines itself when it encounters something stronger. It does not weaken under questioning it clarifies. It becomes more precise, not less certain. Conviction that cannot be questioned is not conviction at all. It is fear dressed as confidence.

Stubbornness and conviction look similar from the outside.
Internally, they are very different.

Conviction is calm.

Stubbornness is tense.

Conviction listens.

Stubbornness defends.

One is grounded in understanding.

The other is grounded in identity protection.

Questioning yourself also humbles the ego in a way nothing else does. It reminds you that your experiences are not universal. That your pain is not exclusive. That your conclusions were shaped by circumstances you did not choose.

The world is too complex to be captured by a single narrative, no matter how convincing it feels.

There is relief in realizing this.

You stop carrying the pressure of being right all the time. You stop interpreting disagreement as disrespect. You stop confusing difference with threat. Instead of reacting, you observe. Instead of defending, you consider. And in that space, thinking deepens.

There is a quiet strength in saying, *I might be wrong.*

That sentence does not shrink you. It expands you. It opens room for correction without collapse. For learning without humiliation. For dialogue without performance. It replaces certainty with curiosity, and curiosity keeps the mind alive.

A mind that questions itself stay alert. It remains capable of revision. It does not fossilize. Without self-questioning, beliefs harden. Once hardened, they stop interacting with reality. They no longer adjust to new information. They persist even when evidence changes.

This is how outdated ideas survive.

Not because they are true, but because they are protected.

The danger of unchallenged belief is not ignorance. It is stagnation. The mind begins repeating instead of thinking. Opinions become reflexes. Responses become predictable. And slowly, thinking gives way to defending what has already been decided.

A mind that never argues with itself eventually stops thinking altogether.

Questioning yourself does not mean living in doubt permanently. It means allowing doubt to pass through when necessary.

Doubt is not paralysis. It is calibration.

It checks alignment. It prevents decay. Without it, certainty grows brittle.

This discipline also changes how you relate to others. Conversations stop being contests.

You are no longer trying to win or convince.

You are trying to understand.

Disagreement becomes less personal. You stop attaching your worth to your position. And because of that, dialogue becomes possible again.

When beliefs are not tied tightly to identity, they can move. When they can move, they can improve.

The individual willing to question themselves is rare, not because it is difficult to think, but because it is difficult to unsettle what feels stable.

It requires sitting with discomfort without resolving it immediately.

It requires admitting that what once made sense may no longer apply.

It requires letting go of certainty before something better

has arrived.

But this discomfort is productive.

It sharpens judgment. It refines perspective.

It replaces inherited certainty with earned understanding. What remains after questioning is not confusion, but clarity that can withstand pressure.

In a world obsessed with being right, the rare strength is honesty with oneself.

Not the honesty of confession, but the honesty of inspection. The willingness to ask whether the ground you are standing on still holds.

Challenge your convictions not to discard them,

but to see if they deserve to remain.

Let disagreement test your ideas.

Let friction reveal their shape.

Because beliefs that survive questioning are not weaker.

They are real.

Beliefs grow stronger when you test them.

-Be More Human-

ACT V
(Alignment)

You Have Your Own Element

A large part of human exhaustion comes from living in borrowed air. Moving through spaces that were never designed to hold you. Adopting timelines, definitions, and expectations that did not grow from your own nature. It often happens quietly. You borrow ideas of success, love, strength, even pain. Not because they feel right, but because they are available.

Accepted. Rewarded.

And then, over time, everything begins to feel heavy.

Effort drains you faster than it should. Progress feels expensive. Living feels like swimming against a current that never softens. You start telling yourself this is normal. That life is supposed to feel like this. That strain is the price of adulthood. But strain is not always resistance. Sometimes it is misplacement.

Every living thing has a state where it moves without force.

Fish do not call water discipline.

Fire does not rehearse how to burn.

Birds do not study flight.

They exist where their nature makes sense.

Movement happens because the environment allows it.

Humans are no different.

But somewhere along the way, adaptation replaced belonging. We learned how to perform well in spaces that slowly suffocated us.

We called it maturity.
We called it adjustment.
We called it growth.

But growth that costs you oxygen is not growth. It is erosion. Slow, invisible, and easily misnamed as strength.

Your element is not a job title. It is not a personality label or a lifestyle aesthetic. It is not something you announce. It is the space where your thinking sharpens instead of dulls. Where your silence feels full rather than empty. Where effort gives something back instead of only taking.

Where you don't need to translate yourself
constantly just to be understood.

In the wrong element, even your strengths begin to turn against you. Sensitivity becomes weakness. Curiosity becomes distraction. Depth becomes "overthinking." Precision becomes rigidity. You start sanding down your edges, not because they are harmful, but because they don't fit the shape of the room. You learn to shrink in socially acceptable ways.

You learn which parts of yourself are tolerated and which
must be hidden.

And the world rewards you for it. That is the dangerous part.

It applauds your ability to survive anywhere. Your flexibility. Your resilience. Your capacity to adjust. What it does not reward is alignment. What it quietly punishes is thriving that does not conform. So, you keep going. You keep adapting. You keep mistaking tolerance for fit.

Until one day, often without planning, you step into the right environment. Nothing about you changes.

Same flaws. Same history. Same doubts.

But the friction disappears. Not completely. Not magically. Just enough to notice.

Effort no longer feels like self-betrayal. Thinking becomes clearer. You speak without rehearsing. You move without apologizing for your pace.

Life feels lighter.

Not easier. Truer.

That is when the realization lands you were never broken. You were misplaced.

This is what makes finding your element difficult to explain. It does not arrive with fireworks. It does not always come with certainty or applause. Often, it arrives as calm. As not needing to prove anything. As your nervous system finally standing down from a long, unnecessary alert.

You stop performing competence. You stop justifying your way of seeing.

You stop arguing with yourself about whether you are too much or not enough.

The inner negotiation quiets because the environment no longer demands it.

And this is where the discomfort enters.

Because once you experience alignment, you cannot unknow it. You can return to old spaces. You can compromise. You can tell yourself you are being practical.

But your body knows the difference between breathing and surviving.

Borrowed air never feels neutral again.

This is why people resist change even when they know something is wrong. Leaving the wrong environment often means losing approval, structure, or familiarity.

Staying means losing yourself slowly.

Both are uncomfortable.

But only one allows you to remain intact.
Finding your element is not escape.

It is recognizing that friction is not always a sign of effort. Sometimes it is a signal of incompatibility. That exhaustion is not always a personal failure. Sometimes it is feedback. That difficulty does not always mean growth. Sometimes it means you are forcing yourself to function where you do not belong.

This does not mean life becomes effortless in the right place. It means effort stops feeling hostile.

It stops eroding you.

It begins to shape you instead of draining you.

Challenges still exist. Doubts still surface. But they do not feel like proof that you are wrong for existing.

What once felt lonely begins to feel honest. What once felt like stagnation begins to feel stable. You stop apologizing for your depth, your pace, your way of processing. You stop trying to be impressive. You start being precise.

The question is not why things feel hard all the time.

The question is whether you are trying to bloom in the wrong climate.

You do not need to become better.

You need to be where you make sense.

And when you are, something quiet and unmistakable happens. You stop fighting yourself. You stop translating your instincts into acceptable language. You stop mistaking survival for success.

What once felt like effort begins to feel like flow.
What once felt heavy begins to feel grounded.

Not because life becomes perfect, but because you finally meet it as yourself.

That is not escape. That is coming home.

You were tired because you were in the wrong place.

-Be More Human-

THE COST Of ALIGNMENT

Alignment is not free.

It asks for things you may not be ready to give. It asks you to walk away from security you have spent years building. It asks you to disappoint people who expected you to stay the same. It asks you to choose uncertainty over comfort, honesty over approval, meaning over money.

And it does not guarantee that the choice will work out.

This is the part that gets left out of most conversations about authenticity. The part where living aligned with yourself costs more than living misaligned. Where doing what feels true leads to isolation, financial instability, and the quiet judgment of people who stayed on the path you left.

No one tells you this upfront. They talk about freedom, purpose, peace. They make it sound like alignment is the natural state you return to once you remove what is false. As if letting go of borrowed ambition automatically leads to stability.

It does not.

What it leads to, often, is loss. Loss of income. Loss of relationships. Loss of the identity you built around doing what was expected. And that loss is real. It is not a metaphor. It is not temporary discomfort on the way to something better.

Sometimes it is permanent.

Sometimes choosing your element means choosing less money for the rest of your life. Sometimes it means watching people you respect lose respect for you. Sometimes it means your family does not understand and never will.

And you need to know this before you make the choice. Because alignment is not a guarantee of ease. It is a trade-off.

You trade external validation for internal coherence. You trade security for honesty. You trade the life that makes sense to others for the life that makes sense to you.

And coherence does not pay rent.

This is why most people know their element and do not choose it. Not because they lack courage, but because they are doing the math. They see what alignment costs and decide the price is too high.

That decision is not cowardice. It is clarity.

Because alignment is not the only valid way to live. Compromise is not betrayal. Choosing security over authenticity does not make you a failure. It makes you someone who weighed the options and chose survival.

There is dignity in that choice. More dignity than most people admit.

The issue is when the choice is not conscious. When you drift into misalignment without noticing. When you build a life that looks successful from the outside but feels hollow from the inside, and you cannot name why.

That is different. That is not strategy. That is erosion.

But when you see the trade-off clearly and choose security anyway, that is not weakness. That is adult decision-making. You are saying: I know my element exists. I know what alignment would require. And I am choosing not to pay that price right now.

That honesty matters. Because it keeps the door open. It prevents bitterness. It allows you to return to the question later, when circumstances change or when the cost of misalignment finally exceeds the cost of alignment.

But if you do choose alignment, you need to go in with your eyes open.

You need to know that it will be harder than you think. That the people who encouraged you to "follow your passion" will not help you pay bills when passion does not convert to income. That the clarity you gain will not make up for the financial instability. That being true to yourself does not make you immune to regret.

Because regret will come. Not regret for the choice itself, but regret for what the choice cost. You will see people who stayed on the traditional path buying houses, taking vacations, building savings. And you will feel the gap. The difference between their stability and your uncertainty.

That gap does not mean you chose wrong. It just means every choice has consequences, and you are living with yours.

Some days, those consequences will feel worth it. You will feel the relief of living honestly. The quiet satisfaction of work that aligns with who you are. The freedom of not performing a role that never fit.

Other days, the consequences will feel unbearable. You will wonder if authenticity was worth this much struggle. If meaning is worth this much instability. If you should have just stayed where you were and learned to tolerate the misalignment.

Both feelings are true. Neither cancels the other out.

This is what makes alignment difficult to hold. It is not a permanent state of peace. It is a constant negotiation between what feels true and what feels sustainable. Between what aligns with your values and what allows you to survive.

Most people expect alignment to resolve that tension. To make the choice feel obvious and clean. But it does not. The tension remains. You just learn to live inside it without letting it collapse you.

And some people cannot live inside that tension. They need more certainty. More stability. More assurance that the sacrifice will be worth it. And when alignment cannot provide that, they return to the path they left.

That return is not failure either. It is honesty. It is the recognition that alignment, for them, at this time, costs more than they can afford to pay.

There is no judgment in that. Only acknowledgment.

Because the truth is, alignment is a privilege. It requires enough safety to take risks. Enough resources to absorb failure. Enough support to survive instability.

Not everyone has that. And pretending everyone does is not wisdom. It is cruelty disguised as inspiration.

If you have the privilege, use it. But do not mistake it for virtue. And do not judge those who cannot afford the cost.

Because the cost is real. And it does not go away just because the choice feels right.

You will lose things. Money. Status. Relationships. The respect of people who mattered to you. The approval of family. The sense that you are doing what you are supposed to do.

And in exchange, you will gain coherence. Honesty. The ability to look at your life and recognize yourself in it. The quiet knowledge that you are not performing someone else's idea of success.

That knowledge will not make the loss hurt less. It will not pay your bills. It will not repair broken relationships. It will not make people understand.

It will just allow you to continue. To keep choosing yourself, even when the cost keeps rising. To stay aligned, even when alignment leads to isolation.

And maybe that is enough. Maybe coherence is worth more than comfort. Maybe honesty is worth more than approval. Maybe meaning is worth more than money.

But maybe it is not. Maybe you need the money. Maybe you need the approval. Maybe you cannot afford to lose what alignment asks you to give up.

And if that is true, you do not need to apologize for it. You do not need to justify staying where you are. You do not need to pretend you are working toward alignment when survival is taking everything you have.

You only need to be honest. With yourself. About what you are choosing and why.

Because the only real betrayal is lying about the choice. Pretending you are aligned when you are not. Pretending you are free when you are trapped. Pretending the cost does not matter when it is quietly destroying you.

The cost always matters. Acknowledge it. Respect it. And then decide if you are willing to pay it.

Not forever. Just for now.

Because alignment is not a final destination. It is a direction. And directions can change when circumstances do.

You are allowed to choose alignment today and choose security tomorrow. You are allowed to try, fail, and return to what is stable. You are allowed to live honestly within your limitations instead of pretending they do not exist.

That honesty is alignment too. Not the romantic version. The real one.

The version that says: I see what this costs. I know what I am giving up. And I am choosing it anyway.

Or: I see what this costs. I cannot pay it right now. And I am choosing stability instead.

Both are true. Both are valid. Both require courage.

The only lie is pretending the cost does not exist. Or that paying it makes you better than those who cannot.

Alignment is not moral superiority. It is a trade-off. And every person gets to decide if the trade is worth it.

Make your choice. Own it. And stop apologizing for what it costs.

The Silence When You Hear YOUR Footsteps

There is a kind of quiet that only appears when you are walking alone.
Not the absence of sound, but the presence of yourself. A silence so precise that it sharpens awareness instead of dulling it. In that space, every footstep becomes audible. Not just to the ear, but to the mind. Each one lands with weight, with intention, with consequence.

This silence does not arrive when you are still.
It arrives when you are moving without witnesses.

There is no crowd to absorb you. No noise to disappear into. No performance to maintain. No applause to lean on. It is just you, your pace, your breath, your direction. You are not reacting. You are choosing. And because of that, the quiet feels different. It does not feel empty.

It feels exact.

Walking alone has a way of revealing what is usually outrun.

When there is no distraction, thoughts no longer scatter. They line up. Not neatly, but honestly. You notice which ones return without being called. You notice which memories still carry weight. You notice which questions have been waiting for space. The rhythm of your steps becomes a kind of anchor.

Each one steady enough to hold whatever rises.

In this quiet, every step forward feels owned.

Not borrowed.
Not inherited.
Not suggested by anyone else's pace.

You move because you decided to move. And that decision repeats itself with every step. Forward becomes something you claim, not something that happens to you. Backward becomes something you acknowledge, not something you deny.

The silence does not judge any of it.

It reflects.

It reminds you that yesterday belongs to you. Not to rewrite, not to escape, but to carry accurately. It reminds you that tomorrow belongs to you as well, not as a promise, but as a responsibility. No one else hears these footsteps the way you do. No one else knows exactly what it took to place them where they are.

The world may still exist at a distance. You can sense it faintly. Movement. Voices. Noise. But it is far enough away to lose authority. Close enough to be real, but distant enough to stop interfering.

What stays near are your footsteps.

Loyal.
Consistent.
Unimpressed.

They do not exaggerate progress.
They do not minimize effort.

They never lie about how far you have come. And they never hide how far you still want to go.

There is something grounding about that honesty.

In this intimacy, silence becomes a teacher. Not one that explains, but one that uncovers. It does not offer answers. It removes interference. It exposes the lessons buried under haste. The moments you rushed past because they did not look impressive. The victories you never acknowledged because no one was there to notice them.

You begin to see that growth was never hiding in noise.

Noise only made it harder to notice.

Growth lived in awareness. In choosing direction without witnesses. In continuing forward without reassurance. In standing upright when no one was watching closely enough to care. The quiet shows you this not as an idea, but as a pattern already lived.

Each step carries proof.

Proof that despite uncertainty, you moved.
Despite doubt, you chose direction.
Despite history, you did not stop.

This is what the silence makes visible. Not courage as an announcement, but courage as persistence. Not clarity a certainty, but clarity as movement without guarantee.

The quiet does not demand confidence.
It only asks for honesty.

And honesty, in this space, becomes unavoidable.

Walking alone also removes comparison. There is no one to match. No one to outrun. No one to fall behind. Your pace is no longer evaluated against another's rhythm. It simply is. Some steps are steady. Some hesitate. Some feel heavier than others.

All of them count.

This is where loneliness is often misunderstood.

The silence does not make you lonely.
It makes you accurate.

It strips away the borrowed energy that comes from being seen and leaves you with what remains when no one is looking. What remains is not emptiness.

It is truth.

Truth about how tired you are.
Truth about how much you can still carry.
Truth about what matters enough to keep moving.

There is grounding in hearing your own footsteps without interruption. In knowing that the sound you are following is yours. Not because it is loud, but because it is consistent.

The quiet allows you to feel the weight of your body, the steadiness of the ground, the simple fact of motion continuing.

You become aware of the person you are becoming, not in theory, but in motion.

Becoming is slow. It does not announce itself. It does not arrive fully formed. It reveals itself through repetition. Through showing up again. Through placing one foot in front of the other even when the destination is unclear.

This is why the silence matters.

It holds the space where becoming happens.

When you walk long enough in this quiet, something settles. The urgency to explain yourself fades. The need to be impressive loosens. You are no longer trying to be understood. You are trying to be aligned.

The difference is subtle. But everything changes because of it.

So, when you hear your own footsteps, let them echo. Let the silence deepen without rushing to fill it. Let it remind you that you are the one carrying this story forward. Not perfectly. Not heroically. But faithfully.

Every step you have taken belongs to you.
Every step ahead is waiting. Not demanding answers.
Asking presence.

The silence is not asking who you should become.
It is asking who you are willing to continue as.
And with each footstep, you answer.

It feels different when the path is yours.

-Be More Human-

People Who Saw Themselves Growing Up

There is a particular kind of clarity that comes from watching yourself change in real time. Not the dramatic, cinematic kind where everything shifts at once, but the quiet recognition that something inside you is no longer arranged the way it used to be. You notice it without ceremony. One day, you realize you are no longer who you were, and not yet who you once imagined you would become.

That in-between space is unfamiliar.
Not confusing. Just honest.

A person who has seen themselves growing up remembers the early days clearly. Not only the events, but the emotional texture of them. The confidence that came before competence. The hunger that existed without direction. The certainty that life would bend easily if you wanted something badly enough.

Back then, mistakes felt temporary. Time felt endless. You believed effort alone was a guarantee. That wanting something sincerely was almost the same as earning it. Consequences existed, but they felt distant, abstract, negotiable.

Growing up begins the moment reality disagrees.

It does not arrive loudly. It does not announce itself as maturity. It shows up through repetition. The same mistakes returning in different forms. The same promises made to yourself, quietly broken. The same patterns circling back when you thought you had outgrown them.

At first, this feels frustrating. Later, it feels instructive.

You begin to learn what enthusiasm cannot replace. Talent without discipline fades. Motivation is unreliable. Consistency matters more than intensity. And eventually, a harder truth settles in: no one is coming to save you. Not from your habits. Not from your delays. Not from the consequences of what you avoid.

This realization does not arrive as a single moment of insight.

It creeps in disguised as exhaustion.

You feel tired of explaining. Tired of blaming. Tired of restarting the same intentions. And somewhere in that fatigue, something shifts. A person who has seen themselves growing up begins to outgrow blame. They stop pointing outward — at circumstances, at parents, at teachers, at society.

Not because those forces did not matter.

But because responsibility is heavier. And more powerful.

Ownership replaces excuses. Not comfortably. Not heroically. But honestly. You realize that even when you were shaped by forces beyond your control, what you do next is still yours to carry. That weight is uncomfortable, but it is grounding. It gives direction where excuses only gave relief.

Growth also brings grief.

This part is rarely acknowledged. You mourn the version of yourself who believed more easily. Who trusted faster. Who dreamed without calculation. You miss the openness, the naivety, the sense that everything was still possible because nothing had been tested yet.

You also begin to lose people.

Not through conflict. Not through dramatic endings. Through silence. Through mismatched rhythms. Through conversations that no longer land the way they once did. You realize some people were chapters, not companions. And you learn, slowly, that outgrowing someone does not make either of you wrong.

It simply means the story moved.

What changes most is your relationship with pain.

Earlier pain felt personal. Failure felt like a verdict on your worth. A confirmation that something about you was lacking. Every setback felt heavier because it was interpreted as meaning something permanent.

Over time, that interpretation changes.
Pain becomes information.

Feedback. A signal that something needs attention or adjustment. You stop asking *why is this happening to me* and start asking *what is this showing me*.

The pain does not become pleasant. But it becomes useful.

This shift alters how you move through the world.

A person who has seen themselves growing up becomes quieter. Not weaker more precise. They speak less because they have learned how easily words can replace action. They stop announcing plans because experience has taught them that execution speaks more clearly than intention.

Confidence moves inward.
Validation becomes optional.

You no longer need to be seen trying. You only need to know that you are doing the work when no one is watching. The desire to impress fades, replaced by the need to be aligned. You become less interested in appearing capable and more interested in being capable.

Another subtle change takes place.
You stop romanticizing the future.

Not because hope disappears, but because
imagination matures.

You understand that becoming someone is not about arrival. It is about alignment. About doing the small, unglamorous things repeatedly. About showing up when motivation is absent. About choosing consistency over excitement.

The future stops being a fantasy and becomes a direction.

You begin respecting the present more. Not because it is perfect, but because it is real. You see how much of life is built here, quietly, without witnesses. You realize how many versions of yourself were formed not by big decisions, but by ordinary days handled with care.

To have seen yourself grow up is not to feel older.
It is to feel grounded.

You carry your past without being controlled by it. You remember who you were without needing to defend or escape that version. You move forward without certainty, but with awareness. And awareness changes everything.

It makes you patient with process.
It makes you honest about limits.
It makes you careful with promises especially the ones you
make to yourself.

You no longer expect life to bend. You learn how to stand.

And that is the quiet strength of someone who has seen
themselves growing up.

Growing up starts when you stop blaming

-Be More Human-

Love Misunderstood.

Those who learned to stay quiet in order to endure often expect understanding without explanation. They grew up in environments where responsibility was felt rather than discussed, where care was demonstrated through provision, consistency, and restraint. Endurance was not just a skill; it was proof of love. Authority was not something to justify. It was something to embody.

In that world, explaining too much felt unnecessary. Sometimes it felt risky. Silence carried meaning. Obedience carried safety. Strength was measured by how much could be carried without complaint, how much could be absorbed without breaking.

Those still becoming are shaped by a different atmosphere.

They are growing up in a world where choice arrives early and relentlessly. Were identity forms in public. Where comparison is constant and narratives multiply faster than certainty. For them, silence does not feel neutral. It feels ambiguous. And ambiguity feels like judgment waiting to happen.

They want to understand before they comply.
They want context before commitment.
They want reassurance where previous generations learned to accept instruction.

This difference is often misread as entitlement or defiance. But it is not rebellion for its own sake. It is self-protection in a world that demands self-definition before stability has fully formed. When guidance arrives without explanation, it feels less like care and more like control. Boundaries feel restrictive not because they are wrong, but because they are unexplained.

Neither side is careless.
Neither side is incapable of strength.

They are responding to different kinds of fear.

Those shaped by scarcity often fear losing control. They have seen what happens when structure collapses. They trust discipline because discipline once kept chaos away. They assume sacrifice will translate into direction, that effort once made will eventually be understood without needing to be spoken aloud.

But unspoken expectations do not create resilience.
They create pressure without shape.

A weight that cannot be named, only carried.

On the other side, those still becoming often fear losing themselves. They push back not to reject love, but to protect autonomy they are still learning how to hold. They are trying to claim space before they fully understand how to inhabit it. Advice, even when sincere, passes through a defensive filter because it feels like a narrowing of possibility.

This is where conversations begin to fracture.

Suggestions start sounding like verdicts.
Questions feel like interrogations.
Concern is heard as criticism.

Pauses grow heavy. Silence fills the space where reassurance should have lived. Over time, misunderstanding becomes the dominant language of the home. Not because anyone intended harm, but because neither side learned how to translate their care into the other's world.

This is not a failure of character.
It is a failure of translation.

A generation that learned strength without emotional vocabulary is now guiding a generation that learned emotional awareness before learning restraint. One learned how to endure without speaking. The other learned how to speak before learning when to pause.

Both learned something real.
Both learned something incomplete.

What's missing is not softer values or louder rebellion. It is not authority giving way to chaos, nor freedom dissolving into disrespect. What's missing is clarity without fear. Expression without threat. Listening without defence.

Not every pause carries disappointment.
Not every boundary is control.
Not every resistance is disrespect.

Sometimes it is just love trying to pass through habits it never evolved beyond.

Understanding does not require agreement. It requires presence. The willingness to remain in the conversation without trying to win it. The willingness to explain without surrendering authority. The willingness to listen without assuming attack.

When expectations are spoken instead of assumed, something shifts. The weight becomes lighter because it finally has shape.

When responses are heard instead of resisted, tension loosens its grip. Not because anyone gave up power, but because both sides stopped misreading each other.

The air in the house changes.
Not dramatically. Quietly.

The distance shortens. Not because perspectives merge, but because they stop colliding. What once felt like opposition begins to feel like difference that can coexist.

The energy moves from defence to recognition.

This was never about authority versus freedom.

It was about time.

About two perspectives shaped under different conditions trying to share the same space. One learned that love survives by holding steady. The other learned that love survives by being expressed. Neither lesson is sufficient on its own.

Healing does not begin with choosing sides.

It begins with asking a different question.

Not *who is right?*
But *what are we failing to hear?*

Most wounds between generations are not caused by love lacking. They are caused by love speaking in languages it never learned to translate.

Love that endured, but never explained.

Love that questioned, but never trusted.

And sometimes, the most difficult work is not changing values, but slowing down enough to hear what was always being offered beneath them.

You See They Won't

No two people live in the same world.

It feels like they do. The same streets, the same conversations, the same events. But reality is never shared the way we assume it is. It is constructed. Filtered. Edited. Each mind builds its own version, shaped by what it fears, what it values, and what it has learned to protect.

That is why a single moment can split into two truths.

To one, it is betrayal.
To another, survival.

To one, it is recklessness.
To another, freedom.

Nothing about the moment itself changes. Only the meaning assigned to it does. And meaning is never neutral. It is assembled from memory, expectation, and unfinished wounds. We don't experience events directly. We experience them through ourselves.

This is where conflict begins.

Perspective is often described as a window, something you look through to see the world. But it works more like a mirror. You don't see reality as it is. You see it reflected through who you are. Your history. Your limits. Your unresolved questions. And when two mirrors face each other, distortion is unavoidable.

Arguments are rarely about facts.
They are collisions of lenses.

Each person believes they are responding to reality. In truth, they are responding to their own reflection. That's why debates feel endless. Why explanations fail. Why being "right" rarely resolves anything. No one is lying. No one is deliberately blind. Each person is living inside a version of the world that feels internally consistent, even when it contradicts someone else's.

This is the part that's uncomfortable to accept.

There is no single world we all inhabit together. There are overlapping realities, layered on top of one another. Close enough to interact. Different enough to clash. Each convincing. Each incomplete. Like dreams unfolding side by side, occasionally brushing against each other, never fully merging.

Understanding this doesn't make conflict disappear. But it changes how you hold it.

You stop trying to win every clash of views. You stop assuming that clarity will arrive if you just explain better, argue longer, or prove harder. You begin to see that disagreement is not always resistance. Sometimes it is orientation. Two people standing in different internal climates, pointing at the same horizon, describing completely different skies.

The shift is subtle. Instead of asking,

how can they not see this?
You start asking, what are they seeing instead?

This doesn't mean abandoning your perspective.

It means loosening your grip on the idea that it must become universal.

The moment you recognize the lens you are looking through; you gain distance from it. And distance is what allows understanding to enter without surrender.

Waking up is not about adopting a superior view.
It's about realizing you were inside one all along.

Once that happens, something changes in how you see others.

They stop looking like obstacles or enemies.

They begin to look like travellers navigating their own internal maps, maps shaped by routes you never walked.

You don’t have to agree with where they are going to recognize that their journey feels real to them.

You see.

They won’t.

Not because they refuse to.
But because they are looking from somewhere else.

They are not wrong
they're just seeing from their perspective.

-Be More Human-

You Were Always Enough

If you've made it here, you weren't searching for answers.

Something in you recognized itself along the way. Not dramatically. Not as relief. Just as that faint echo that keeps you turning pages when you're not sure why.

You didn't read this to become different. You read it to see if someone else had noticed the same things you were afraid to name.

Life didn't shift while you were reading. The world didn't pause. People remained tangled. Days still carried weight. Nothing on the surface changed. But maybe, without announcing itself, the way you looked at it all tilted slightly.

Not enough to feel like breakthrough. Just enough to notice.

Maybe you caught yourself rushing your own thoughts. Maybe you noticed how often you slip out of moments before they've had a chance to settle. How easily attention drifts toward what comes next instead of staying with what's already here. How much effort goes into being "enough" and how little is given to simply being present.

This book wasn't trying to improve you.

It wasn't offering tools or instructions or a cleaner version of yourself to aim for. It only wanted to slow you down long enough to notice where you were already human, before you tried to become anything else.

Most days will still feel ordinary. That isn't a problem. That's where life happens. Not in moments that announce their importance, but in the ones that pass unnoticed unless you're there to meet them.

Meaning doesn't arrive like a revelation. It grows quietly, through small choices—the words you choose when you could stay silent, the moments you don't rush past, the times you let something soften instead of tightening against it.

If something from these pages stayed with you, you don't need to define it. You don't need to protect it or apply it correctly.

Just let it walk alongside you.

Soon enough, life will speed up again. The noise will return. Expectations will close in. You'll be pulled back into schedules, comparisons, responsibilities, and the quiet pressure to perform yourself convincingly.

When that happens, don't expect the ideas to hold. You'll forget most of what you read. That's fine. What matters isn't what you remember, but what you do when you forget.

When noise returns and you lose yourself in it will you notice?

When you start performing again will you catch yourself?

When alignment feels too costly and you choose security instead will you do it consciously, or will you drift?

The answers aren't here. They're in the days ahead. In the moments when philosophy meets reality and only one of them survives.

You already know which one that will be.

So don't expect the ideas to hold. Expect yourself to forget them. Expect life to be harder than reflection. Expect the gap between knowing and doing to remain.

And then, in the middle of that gap, take one honest step.

Not toward becoming better.

Just toward being here.

Awake. Present. Human.

That step won't feel like progress. It will feel ordinary.

Small. Insufficient.

Take it anyway.

Progress was never the point. Presence was. And you were always capable of that. You just forgot to give yourself permission.

So here it is, one last time.

You're allowed to be exactly who you are right now. Struggling. Uncertain. Trying. Failing. Continuing anyway.

Not because you're working toward something better.

You are not broken machinery waiting for the right manual. You are not behind. You are not missing some essential piece that everyone else was given. You're not failing at being human.

You're human. Exactly as complicated and contradictory as that implies.

What you read here wasn't instruction. It was reflection. A mirror held up so you could see what you've been carrying without realizing it. The noise you mistook for thought. The performance you mistook for connection. The fear you mistook for wisdom.

None of it was wrong. It was just automatic. And automatic living, when it continues long enough, stops feeling like living at all.

So, you slowed down. You noticed. You questioned. You allowed discomfort instead of immediately rushing to resolve it and in that space, something became visible that was always there but rarely seen.

You. Not the version you perform. Not the one you hope to become. Just you. Unfinished. Uncertain. Trying.

That version doesn't need to become anything else before it's allowed to exist.

You've spent most of your life being handed definitions of what it means to be enough. Achieve this. Earn that. Look like this. Think like that. Be productive. Be resilient. Be mindful. Be better.

Better than what? Better than who you are right now?
That premise is the trap.

It suggests that who you are right now is insufficient. That presence, awareness, effort none of it counts unless it produces transformation. That simply being isn't valuable unless it's moving toward becoming.

But becoming what?

The person you think you should be? The person others expect? The person who finally has it together, who no longer struggles, who moves through life without friction or doubt?

That person doesn't exist.

And chasing them is what keeps you from inhabiting who you already are.

You don't need to wake up tomorrow and live differently.

You don't need new routines, new rules, or a different set of beliefs to carry forward.

There is no version of you that needs to be assembled from what you've read.

All it ever asked for was your attention.

And if everything else fades, if the chapters blur together and the sentences no longer stand out, let this remain quietly intact.

You were never behind.

You were just learning how to stand up without losing yourself. That work continues tomorrow

In the end, what makes us human is not how long we lived, but how fully we were present while we were here.

Be More Human

To moments that passed quietly, yet stayed forever.
To weight I carried without ever naming it.
To mistakes that closed certain doors and opened better ones.
To people who walked beside me for a while, and the ones who still do.
To silence that never felt empty, only honest.
To the discipline that held me steady
when emotions couldn't.
To versions of me that ended so this one could exist.
To mom, open-hearted, endlessly giving, working through everything with a smile that made hard days feel lighter.
To dad, steady, positive, and strong in a way that never needed to be announced, only lived.
To di equal parts warmth, honesty, and quiet support that always showed up when it mattered (*mastermind)*
To the journey that never promised ease,
only meaning.
And to you, reading this for being here, quietly, at the same point in time as me.

To Being More Human

I’ll write more, don’t you ever forget!!!!!

Founder of

CONCEPT X

SEWCHIC.

Be More Human

And many more…